REDEFINING FINANCIAL ECOSYSTEMS IN ASIA AND THE PACIFIC

A NEW ERA OF OPEN BANKING, OPEN FINANCE, AND INCLUSIVE GROWTH

DECEMBER 2024

ASIAN DEVELOPMENT BANK

 Creative Commons Attribution 3.0 IGO license (CC BY 3.0 IGO)

© 2024 Asian Development Bank
6 ADB Avenue, Mandaluyong City, 1550 Metro Manila, Philippines
Tel +63 2 8632 4444; Fax +63 2 8636 2444
www.adb.org

Some rights reserved. Published in 2024.

ISBN 978-92-9277-059-4 (print); 978-92-9277-060-0 (PDF); 978-92-9277-061-7 (ebook)
Publication Stock No. TCS240572-2
DOI: http://dx.doi.org/10.22617/TCS240572-2

The views expressed in this publication are those of the authors and do not necessarily reflect the views and policies of the Asian Development Bank (ADB) or its Board of Governors or the governments they represent.

ADB does not guarantee the accuracy of the data included in this publication and accepts no responsibility for any consequence of their use. The mention of specific companies or products of manufacturers does not imply that they are endorsed or recommended by ADB in preference to others of a similar nature that are not mentioned.

By making any designation of or reference to a particular territory or geographic area in this document, ADB does not intend to make any judgments as to the legal or other status of any territory or area.

This publication is available under the Creative Commons Attribution 3.0 IGO license (CC BY 3.0 IGO) https://creativecommons.org/licenses/by/3.0/igo/. By using the content of this publication, you agree to be bound by the terms of this license. For attribution, translations, adaptations, and permissions, please read the provisions and terms of use at https://www.adb.org/terms-use#openaccess.

This CC license does not apply to non-ADB copyright materials in this publication. If the material is attributed to another source, please contact the copyright owner or publisher of that source for permission to reproduce it. ADB cannot be held liable for any claims that arise as a result of your use of the material.

Please contact pubsmarketing@adb.org if you have questions or comments with respect to content, or if you wish to obtain copyright permission for your intended use that does not fall within these terms, or for permission to use the ADB logo.

Corrigenda to ADB publications may be found at http://www.adb.org/publications/corrigenda.

Notes:
In this publication, "$" refers to United States dollars and "S$" refers to Singapore dollars.
ADB recognizes "Hong Kong" as Hong Kong, China; "Korea" as the Republic of Korea; and "Vietnam" as Viet Nam.

Cover design by Cleone Flores Baradas.

 Printed on recycled paper

Contents

Acknowledgments

This technical paper on open finance was prepared as part of the support of the Asian Development Bank (ADB) to knowledge work on digital financial services among its developing member countries.

We would like to thank Ramesh Subramaniam, director general and group chief, Sectors Group and Christine Engstrom, senior sector director of Finance Sector Office, Sectors Group (SG-FIN) for their support and guidance in the crafting of this report. The initial draft was authored by Zennon Kapron and Sivapriya Anbarasu who provided the expertise and knowledge for developing this report. They also led the refining work of the report with comments and inputs from colleagues in ADB and external reviewers. Yonghwi Kwon, financial sector specialist (digital payment), SG-FIN led the development and production of the report. Lisette Cipriano, principal digital finance specialist, SG-FIN provided overall directions, valuable feedback, and inputs, and supervised its production. Special thanks go to Grigory McKain, research affiliate, University of Cambridge, who served as peer reviewer without sparing the hard effort. Their invaluable advice helped enhance the quality and the proper structure of the report. We are most grateful for their patience, feedback, and advice. We also appreciate the inputs of Gyeong Chan Jung, senior manager, Korea Financial Telecommunications and Clearings Institute, for comments and insights from his experiences in the open finance project in the Republic of Korea.

The report was produced with the support of a team of Ozden Onturk, financial sector specialist, ADB consultants, and Eric Van Zant as editor. Katherine Mitzi Co, associate operations analyst, SG-FIN and Matilde Mila Cauinian, operations assistant, SG-FIN provided valuable administrative support. ADB greatly acknowledges all these contributions.

Abbreviations

ADB	Asian Development Bank
AI	artificial intelligence
API	application programming interfaces
ASEAN	Association of Southeast Asian Nations
BSP	Bangko Sentral ng Pilipinas
DBS	Development Bank of Singapore
eKYC	electronic know-your-customer
EU	European Union
HKMA	Hong Kong Monetary Authority
KYC	know-your-customer
MAS	Monetary Authority of Singapore
PSD2	Payment Services Directive 2
SGFinDex	Singapore Financial Data Exchange
SMEs	small and medium-sized enterprises
UK	United Kingdom
UPI	unified payments interface

Executive Summary

This report, *Redefining Financial Ecosystems in Asia and the Pacific: A New Era of Open Banking, Open Finance, and Inclusive Growth*, examines the evolution, current state, and prospects of open finance, emphasizing its potential to drive financial inclusion in Asia and the Pacific.

Open banking is the exchange of consumer data among financial service providers and third-party providers. Open finance expands on the principles of open banking, encompassing a broader range of financial services, including mortgages, investments, pensions, and insurance.

Open finance is built on four key components: data sharing, customer consent, insights generation, and actionable outcomes. The technical foundation of open finance relies on application programming interfaces, which facilitate secure and efficient data exchange.

The promise of open finance lies in its significant potential for improving financial inclusion, especially in developing economies. Key use cases include alternative credit scoring for underserved populations, embedded lending and insurance services, streamlined payment systems, and smart onboarding processes. These innovations can lead to more accessible and tailored financial products, particularly for individuals and small and medium-sized enterprises traditionally excluded from the formal financial system.

In Asia and the Pacific, the adoption of open finance varies significantly across economies. Economies such as Malaysia, Singapore, Thailand, and Viet Nam have adopted market-driven approaches. Australia has implemented a regulator-mandated approach, while the Philippines and Hong Kong, China have opted for regulator-guided approaches.

Despite progress, comprehensive implementation of open finance is still in its early stages across the region. Successful implementation of open finance requires common standards for interoperability, measures to ensure industry readiness, robust security standards and practices, consumer education to build trust, incentives for participation in market-led regimes, inclusive policy frameworks, and the building of cross-border synergies.

In addition, the integration of open finance faces technical challenges, particularly in modernizing legacy banking systems. To tackle this, three main approaches have emerged: complete system overhaul, gradual phased transition, and building parallel, cloud-native platforms. Cultural considerations are also crucial for successful adoption, including adapting to local financial behaviors, addressing data privacy concerns, and ensuring accessibility for diverse populations.

Open finance presents a transformative opportunity for the financial sector, particularly in driving financial inclusion. The future of open finance will be shaped by the evolving roles of traditional financial institutions and tech giants, comprehensive regulatory frameworks, collaborative ecosystems fostering innovation, investment in digital literacy and financial education, international cooperation and harmonization of standards, and phased implementation strategies. As Asia and the Pacific navigate this evolving landscape, a thoughtful and adaptive approach will help realize the full potential of open finance.

I. Introduction

The concept of open banking has recently garnered significant attention in the financial industry. Fueled by rapid technological advancement and evolving consumer expectations, open banking represents a paradigm shift that moves beyond traditional banking frameworks to offer a potentially more inclusive, efficient, and innovative approach to financial services.[1]

Fundamentally, open banking is a system in which the consumer data banks hold is shared through application programming interfaces (APIs) with third-party providers, with customers' consent, to create new or improved financial products and services. Open finance expands upon the concept of open banking by incorporating a broader range of financial services and data-sharing capabilities.

Imagine a scenario where a person has multiple bank accounts, each with its own login credentials and interface. Instead of the hassle of navigating through these disparate platforms, open banking enables the creation of a centralized dashboard that consolidates all the account information in one place.

Through the power of API integrations and secure data sharing with the customer's consent, this dashboard provides a comprehensive view of the user's financial profile. Gone are the days of juggling multiple logins and struggling to keep track of balances across different institutions. Through its account aggregation use case, open banking empowers individuals to have a holistic understanding of their financial standing, allowing them to make more informed decisions and better manage their money.

This broadening of open banking into open finance enables a more seamless, interconnected financial ecosystem where data sharing and consumer consent are central. By integrating data from various financial institutions and nonfinancial entities, open finance enables a more holistic view of an individual's economic health. Moreover, open finance apps give customers access to a marketplace of financial services, including instant savings and investment products, enabling them to move their money around more efficiently and potentially access better returns, loans, or insurance products.

This functionality is facilitated by the payment message standards integrated into many open finance regulations, allowing firms with a payments license to act as brokers, making payments from a customer's account to other financial services providers, such as investment accounts. Thus, open finance is not only about opening information flows but also about opening payment systems and reducing friction for customers who want to move their money between different financial service providers seamlessly.

---

[1] The terms open banking and open finance are used extensively throughout this report. As detailed in the report, there are clear differences between the two concepts, but in the industry, they are often incorrectly used interchangeably. As much as possible, this paper has been very specific about referring to one, the other, or both, although there might be overlap in certain cases.

Open data, in turn, extends to the concept of open finance, which signifies the integration of a wide range of data from different sectors, including health care, utilities, social media, etc., in addition to financial data. Such integration fosters a more competitive and innovative financial industry where services can be customer-focused, tailored to meet the diverse needs of consumers and businesses, and especially help individuals and micro, small and medium-sized enterprises (SMEs) in underserved segments of the market by creating low-cost financial services. The rapid advancement of technology is a critical driver in the evolution of open banking and open finance, with innovations such as widespread digitalization and artificial intelligence (AI) laying the groundwork for this new financial paradigm. AI, for instance, can leverage vast amounts of data to provide personalized financial advice and automate processes, improving customer experiences and operational efficiency. Meanwhile, the ubiquity of mobile internet access has helped make financial services more accessible, allowing users to manage their finances anytime and anywhere.

The regulatory environment also plays a crucial role in facilitating and governing the implementation of open banking across Asia. Governments and regulatory bodies have proactively adopted legal and standards frameworks to support the secure sharing of financial data while ensuring consumer protection and fostering innovation. Key initiatives include:

- the United Kingdom's (UK) Open Banking Implementation Entity mandating security standards and industry guidelines;
- the European Union's Payment Services Directive 2 (PSD2) and Berlin Group's technical standards;
- Australia's Consumer Data Rights legislation, with strict security and privacy rules;
- Singapore's guidelines and API adoption initiatives;
- Hong Kong, China's Open API framework with phased security controls; and
- Brazil's regulatory framework overseen by the central bank alongside industry-led technical standards.

These regulatory reforms aim to create a balanced ecosystem where traditional banks, fintech startups, and nonfinancial entities can collaborate and compete. By establishing clear technology, data privacy, cybersecurity, and consent management guidelines and standards, regulators are laying the groundwork for a sustainable open banking and open finance infrastructure that promotes transparency, efficiency, and inclusivity in the financial sector.

The advancement of open finance could provide substantial benefits across the financial ecosystem and value chain. Customers, whether retail or business, have easier access to more innovative and economic products and services. Banks and incumbents can tap into new revenue streams as well as focus on their core business. Fintech firms are able to more easily accessing banking products and services, potentially without the need for a complex on-boarding process. Finally, policymakers and regulators can both increase access to financial products and services and stimulate market competition.

However, it is also important to acknowledge the arguments against open finance, such as the potential development of unsuitable products, the increased burden on regulators to supervise more entities, and the risk of primarily benefiting customers who are already financially well-off. There are concerns that smaller financial institutions may struggle to keep up with technological demands, and that increased competition could drive down profits for incumbents.

Despite the promising potential of open finance in Asia, the journey toward a fully integrated and inclusive financial ecosystem also faces several challenges. Digital literacy and infrastructure disparities across the region can hinder the accessibility and effectiveness of open finance solutions. Data privacy and security concerns also pose significant obstacles to consumer trust and participation. In addition, although many jurisdictions have agreed on common open banking standards and frameworks, the challenge is now harmonizing those standards and ensuring interoperability.

However, these challenges also present opportunities for innovation, regulatory evolution, and collaborative efforts to build a more robust, secure, and inclusive financial landscape. Addressing these issues is critical for realizing open finance's full potential in fostering economic growth and financial inclusion.

This report examines the potential for open finance to enable financial inclusion and help the financial ecosystem, regulators, and market participants across Asia and the Pacific to understand its transformative potential. By dissecting the mechanisms, benefits, and challenges of open banking and open finance, the report serves as a guide for leveraging this innovative framework to create a more inclusive, efficient, and equitable financial landscape, ultimately contributing to the region's socioeconomic development.

Open Finance: A Definition

Before defining open finance, it is helpful to understand the concept of open banking.

Open banking is defined as "the exchange of consumer data between banks and other financial service providers, on the basis of customer consent, with other financial service providers and Third-Party Providers such as fintechs."[2] It refers to enabling third-party access to specific banking data such as current and savings account information, card accounts, loans, and know-your-customer (KYC) information, enabling the creation of new financial services and products by third parties.

Historically, banks have maintained exclusive control over customer data, giving them a built-in advantage in developing new products and services. However, a significant portion of this data has been siloed within disparate systems and processes within banks and thus is often underutilized. Additionally, banks have always prioritized stability and compliance over customer experience, which can stifle innovation. With open banking, third-party providers (i.e., data users) can leverage this data held by the banks, with customer consent, to create new products and services that enhance usage and experience, often lowering costs and increasing efficiency. Hence, open banking aims to increase competition and innovation within the banking sector.

While open banking enables third-party access to some traditional banking data, open finance extends the scope of open banking to all financial data, encompassing a broader spectrum of financial services such as mortgages, investments, pensions, and insurance. Thus, it aims for a more integrated and comprehensive financial ecosystem.

The Components of Open Finance

While businesses, regulatory bodies, and governments have adopted a variety of frameworks to encourage and regulate data sharing in the financial sector, the majority of these approaches require these four critical components: data, consent, insights, and action.[3]

---

[2]   A. Plaitakis, and S. Staschen. 2020. Open Banking: How to Design for Financial Inclusion. *Working Paper*. CGAP.
https://www.cgap.org/sites/default/files/publications/2020_10_Working_Paper_Open_Banking.pdf.

[3]   Basiq. *Visualising an Open Finance Ecosystem*. White paper. https://basiq.io/white-papers/basiq-visualising-an-open-finance-ecosystem.pdf.

Data. At the heart of open banking and open finance lies the principle of data sharing. This involves the exchange of financial information, traditionally guarded under strict client confidentiality clauses by banks, under a new paradigm emphasizing transparency and accessibility.[4] Data sharing enables the flow of customer financial information across entities, laying the groundwork for personalized financial solutions.

Consent. Central to ensuring privacy and trust in the open finance ecosystem is consent. This principle addresses the critical need for customer approval before their personal and financial data can be shared or used. It requires explicit authorization from customers to both data providers and users, including third-party providers, thereby safeguarding personal information and aligning with legal standards for data privacy.

Insights. With customer consent to access data, service providers proceed to derive insights from the shared information. This step involves analyzing financial behaviors, patterns, and transactions to gain a deep understanding of the customer's financial health, preferences, and needs. Insights drawn from data analysis can inform creditworthiness assessments, financial planning, and the development of tailored financial products and services.

Action. The final component, action, encapsulates the application of insights gained from data analysis. Actions may include financial decisions or operations taken on behalf of the customer, such as facilitating payments, offering personalized financial advice, or integrating customer data into third-party platforms for enhanced financial management. This actionable phase is where the tangible benefits of the open finance ecosystem manifest, directly impacting the consumer's financial experience and opportunities.

Technical Requirements

From a technical perspective, secure and efficient data sharing under informed consent is enabled by APIs. An API is "a set of rules or protocols that let software applications communicate with each other to exchange data, features, and functionality."[5] Open APIs are proprietary APIs that a financial service provider makes widely available for other companies to consume, allowing these other companies to seamlessly plug into the provider's system to access their customer's financial information, such as transaction history, bank account details, and credit statements (footnote 2).

Open banking APIs typically come in two types:

- **Read-only access.** Third-party providers that have read-only access to a customer's financial information can view the data but cannot make any changes. This access might be used for services that analyze spending patterns or offer financial advice without altering the account details or initiating transactions.
- **Read + Write Access.** In addition to viewing customer data, third-party providers with read + write access can modify or interact with it. This could involve initiating transactions such as transfers or payments on behalf of the customer.

---

[4]   World Bank. 2021. *Technical Note: The Role of Consumer Consent in Open Banking. Financial Inclusion Support Framework.* https://documents1.worldbank.org/curated/en/099425002082230437/pdf/P1705050aeb8e704f088260f228802b73b8.pdf.
[5]   International Business Machines Corporation (IBM). What Is an Application Programming Interface? https://www.ibm.com/topics/api.

Figure 1 illustrates the concept.

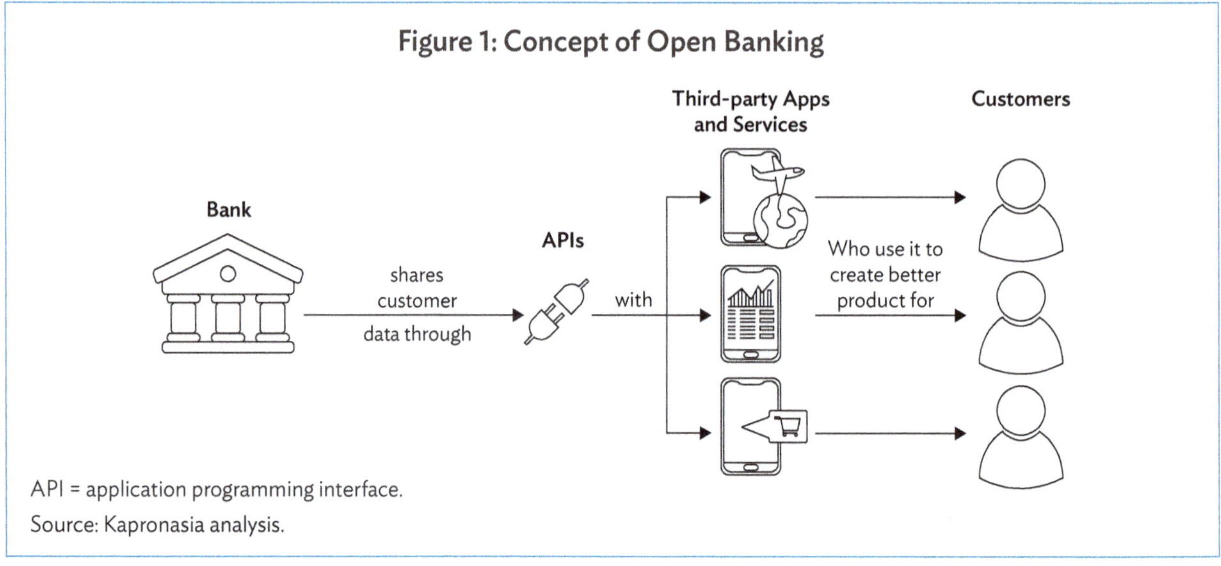

Figure 1: Concept of Open Banking

API = application programming interface.

Source: Kapronasia analysis.

Open Finance Versus Open Data

Just as open finance extends from open banking, "open data" builds on open finance. Open data, a much broader and related concept, refers to data that is freely available to everyone to use and redistribute as they wish, without restrictions from copyright, patents, or other mechanisms of control.[6] While open finance focuses specifically on the financial sector, open data can encompass a wide range of data from different sectors, including healthcare, utilities, social media, etc.

Open data is often anonymized and general, as opposed to open finance, which deals with personal and sensitive financial information and necessitates stringent security and privacy measures.

In summary, all three concepts—open banking, open finance, and open data—are closely related, building on each other with similar underlying principles. However, this report focuses on open banking and open finance. Box 1 presents a case study from the UK on the use of open date.

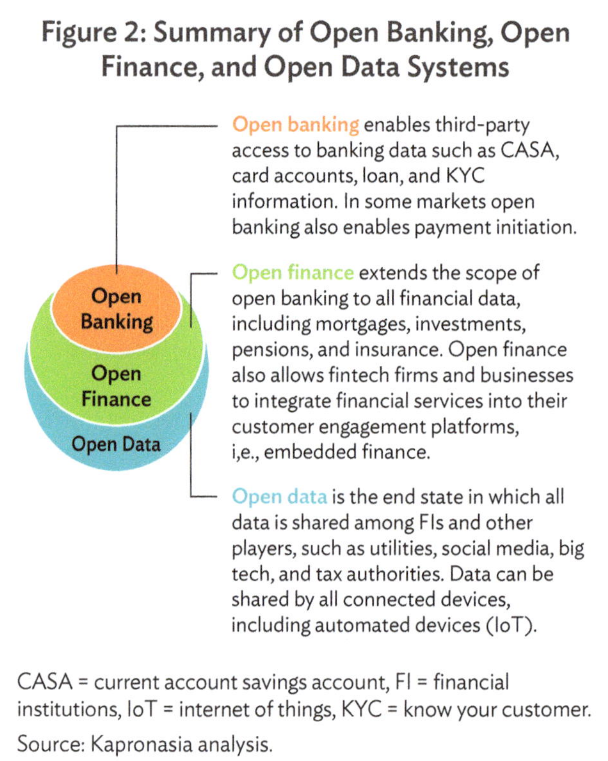

Figure 2: Summary of Open Banking, Open Finance, and Open Data Systems

Open banking enables third-party access to banking data such as CASA, card accounts, loan, and KYC information. In some markets open banking also enables payment initiation.

Open finance extends the scope of open banking to all financial data, including mortgages, investments, pensions, and insurance. Open finance also allows fintech firms and businesses to integrate financial services into their customer engagement platforms, i,e., embedded finance.

Open data is the end state in which all data is shared among FIs and other players, such as utilities, social media, big tech, and tax authorities. Data can be shared by all connected devices, including automated devices (IoT).

CASA = current account savings account, FI = financial institutions, IoT = internet of things, KYC = know your customer.
Source: Kapronasia analysis.

---

6   Open Data Handbook. What is Open Data? https://opendatahandbook.org/guide/en/what-is-open-data/.

Box 1: Case Study of Open Data in United Kingdom Transport

An example of where open banking, open finance, and open data have converged is in the collaboration between the United Kingdom's transport sector and fintech companies. One notable instance is the partnership between Transport for London and various fintech firms to leverage open data for innovative solutions. Transport for London, an early mover in open data sharing, provides real-time transport information to developers, enabling the creation of apps that enhance the commuter experience and facilitate seamless payments.

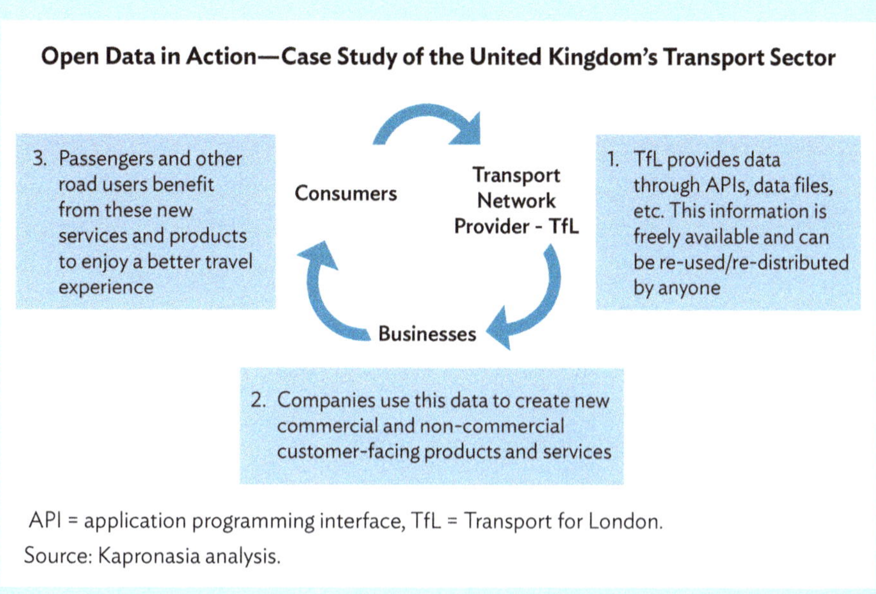

API = application programming interface, TfL = Transport for London.
Source: Kapronasia analysis.

Integration and Implementation:

Integration begins with fintech companies developing applications that access both open data from public transportation databases and utilize open banking application programming interface for payment processing. These applications can, for example, calculate the best fare for a commuter's journey across multiple modes of transport (bus, train, tram) in real-time, considering the day's travel patterns and the individual's travel history.

Commuters benefit from a seamless travel experience where fares are dynamically calculated and paid for through the app, without needing to purchase tickets in advance or carry cash. This system also supports pay-as-you-go and caps fares to ensure commuters always get the best value based on their actual travel.

Impact:

- **Enhanced convenience.** Commuters enjoy a hassle-free travel experience with automated best-price fare calculations and easy account-based payments.
- **Increased efficiency.** Public transport operators can optimize services based on the rich insights derived from the integration of travel data and payment behaviors.
- **Innovation and personalization.** Open data allows development of new services and features, such as personalized travel recommendations or alerts.

Sources: Department for International Trade. 2019. UK FinTech State of the Nation. https://assets.publishing.service.gov.uk/media/5cd9511740f0b62d81cad294/UK-fintech-state-of-the-nation.pdf; Zandamela. 2021. The Benefits of Open Banking to Consumers, Banks and FinTech Companies. Sheffield Hallam University Research Archive. https://shura.shu.ac.uk/30227/1/Zandamela_2021_DBA_BenefitsOpenBanking.pdf.

Historical Context of Open Finance

The origins of open finance can be traced back to the emergence of open banking, whose genesis arose out of legislation known as the Second Payment Services Directive, or PSD2, in 2016. The directive aimed to (i) promote innovation and competition in retail payments, (ii) enhance payment security, and (iii) protect consumer data. The European Union (EU) member states were given until January 2018 to transpose it into respective national laws.[7]

Following this, the UK's Competition and Markets Authority mandated the development of an "open-banking standard" by requiring the country's nine biggest banks to share customer and transaction data with third parties through APIs, provided the customers had given their consent. This was a revolutionary idea, aiming to break the monopoly of traditional banks over customer data and open the market to fintech companies, thus fostering competition and innovation. As of December 2020, the UK had issued some 200 third-party provider licenses for open-banking APIs.[8]

As open banking began to take root, its potential for transforming banking and potentially the entire financial services sector became evident. The seamless and secure sharing of financial data across different service providers heralded a new era of financial inclusivity and innovation, extending beyond the confines of traditional banking. This realization marked the conceptual expansion toward open finance.

Rapid technological advancements and changing consumer expectations, coupled with the widespread adoption of internet and mobile technology, propelled the evolution toward open finance. Consumers, accustomed to the convenience and personalization offered by digital platforms in other areas of their lives, began to demand the same from their financial services. This shift in consumer behavior underscored the need for a more flexible, responsive, and integrated financial ecosystem.

At the same time, the General Data Protection Regulation, a comprehensive data protection law introduced by the EU in 2018, played a crucial role in shaping the open banking and open finance landscape by emphasizing data privacy and consumer control over personal information. The regulation reinforced the principles of data ownership and consent, aligning with the core tenets of open banking and open finance.

While the initial push for open banking and, subsequently, open finance originated in Europe, the concept gained traction globally. Economies across Asia, Africa, and the Americas began to explore and implement their versions of open banking and open finance, each adapting the model to fit their unique regulatory, economic, and cultural contexts.

---

[7]   European Central Bank. 2018. The Revised Payment Services Directive (PSD2) and the Transition to Stronger Payments Security. https://www.ecb.europa.eu/press/intro/mip-online/2018/html/1803_revisedpsd.en.html.

[8]   C. Asif, T. Olanrewaju, H. Sayama, and A. Vijayasrinivasan. 2021. Financial Services Unchained: The Ongoing Rise of Open Financial Data. McKinsey & Company. https://www.mckinsey.com/industries/financial-services/our-insights/financial-services-unchained-the-ongoing-rise-of-open-financial-data.

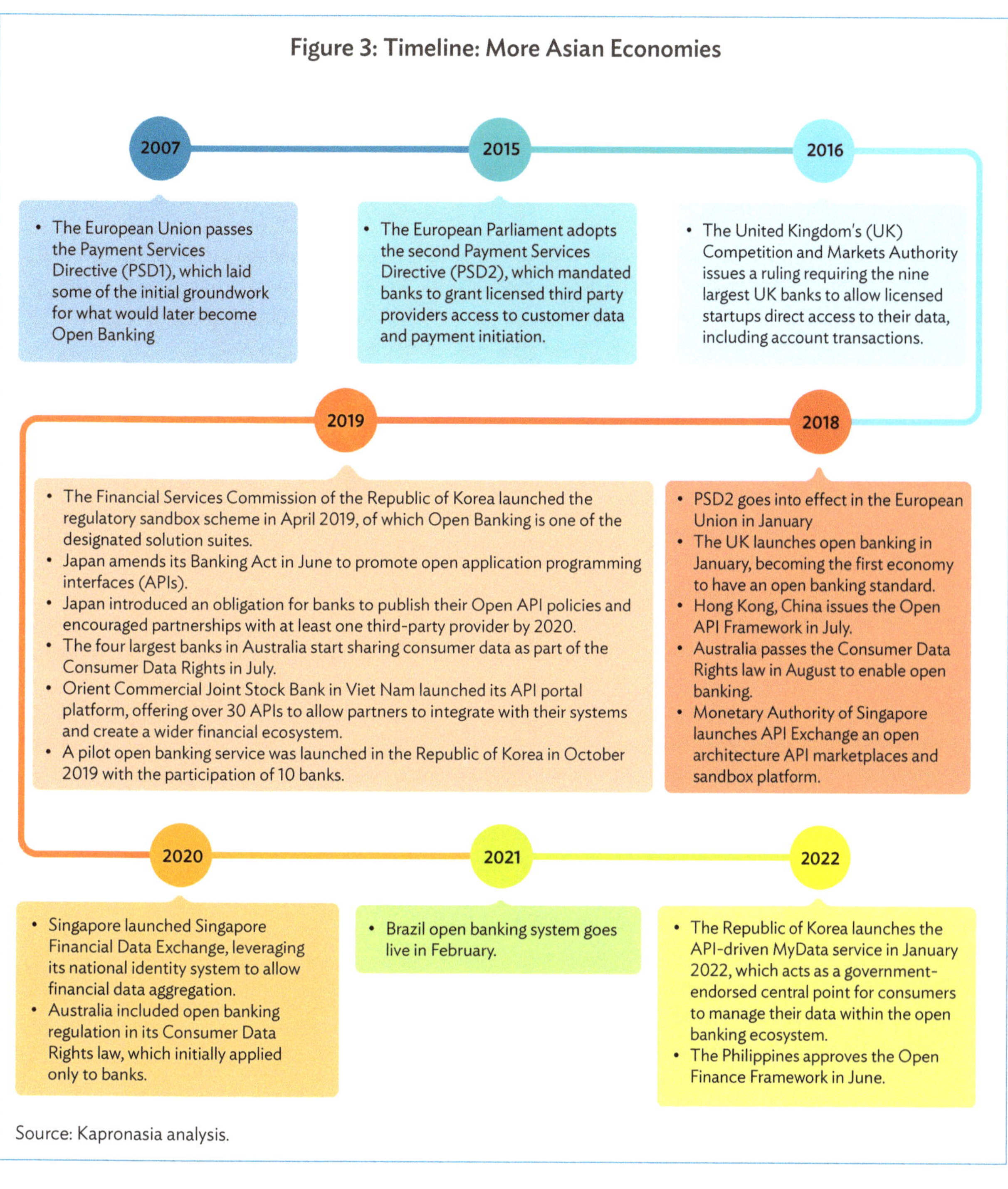

Source: Kapronasia analysis.

Stakeholders in the Open Finance Ecosystem

The very idea of open banking and open finance requires an ecosystem of participants who work together in various capacities. From traditional financial institutions to regulatory bodies and fintech innovators, and each plays a crucial part in shaping the evolving landscape of open finance. Understanding these stakeholders is essential for grasping the complexities and opportunities.

Data owners are the central figures in the open finance ecosystem. They own the financial data and provide consent for its use across the ecosystem. The data owners are typically also the end customers and can be individual consumers or businesses, including SMEs. Data owners in an open finance ecosystem typically benefit from increased convenience, personalized services, and greater financial control.

Data providers hold a customer's financial information (account balances, transaction history, credit scores, etc.) and can securely share this data with other ecosystem participants with customer consent. The data providers can be banks and other financial service providers such as credit unions, investment firms, etc.

Data users are often fintech companies or other third-party service providers who, with permission, leverage the shared consumer data from the providers to offer a wide range of innovative financial products and services. Examples of users might include account aggregators, platforms, and payment solution providers. These services can either be embedded or provided as stand-alone services.

Data intermediaries or API aggregators provide a unified interface for accessing and aggregating data from various financial institution APIs (footnote 8). Intermediaries and aggregators do not directly offer financial products or services and only serve as a middle layer, primarily facilitating data access for other data users. Because of their role as technology providers, intermediaries are also not typically required to have any special license to operate, as they are not processing payments or handling funds.

Regulators are tasked with creating and enforcing policies that promote innovation, protect consumer rights and data security, enhance market competition, and ensure overall financial stability. Regulatory frameworks ensure that data sharing respects consumer privacy and data protection laws, establishing the necessary trust for consumers to participate willingly in the open finance ecosystem.

Open Banking and Open Finance Use Cases

Numerous factors call for open banking and open finance. Just a few of these use cases include:

(i)   **Account aggregation.** Allowing users to view all their bank accounts from multiple institutions in a single dashboard, enabling better financial management.

(ii)   **Personal finance management.** Providing users with personalized financial insights, budgeting tools, and savings recommendations based on their transaction data.

(iii) **Simplified loan applications.** Enabling users to share their financial data with lenders directly, streamlining the loan application process, and potentially improving access to credit.

(iv)   **Automated accounting.** Integrating banking data with accounting software, reducing manual data entry, and simplifying bookkeeping for businesses.

(v)   **Fraud detection.** Analyzing transaction data across multiple accounts to identify potential fraud and protect users from financial crime.

(vi)   **Payments initiation.** Allowing third-party providers to initiate payments directly from a user's bank account, providing an alternative to card payments.

(vii)   **Personalized product recommendations.** Analyzing users' financial data to offer tailored product recommendations, such as savings accounts, credit cards, or insurance policies.

(viii)   **Wealth management.** Providing users with a comprehensive view of their investments across multiple institutions, offering personalized advice and investment options through embedded investing.

(ix)   **Subscription management.** Helping users track and manage their subscriptions and recurring payments, identifying opportunities to save money.

(x)   **Identity verification.** Using bank account data to verify a user's identity, streamlining onboarding processes for financial services, and reducing fraud risk.

Many of the use cases listed above and detailed later in this report are usable by both individuals and businesses, often with very similar elements, but varying goals. An example of account aggregation use case is outlined in Box 2.

Box 2: Account Aggregation and Analysis

As digital banks, wallets, and other financial platforms have proliferated, it has become increasingly challenging for consumers and businesses to have a holistic view of all their finances in one place. This complexity makes it difficult to effectively have a financial plan.

The Account Aggregation Open Finance use case enables a consumer or business to aggregate all of their holdings in one place. The Singapore Financial Data Exchange (SGFinDex) is a good example of how this can work in practice.

The Monetary Authority of Singapore-sponsored SGFinDex platform interconnects customer data from across banks and allows aggregation in one place. A Development Bank of Singapore user, for example, can log in and see all their finances in one portal. The platform allows individuals and businesses to have a consolidated view of their financial accounts across different institutions. By offering a holistic view of finances, it aids in better financial planning and management.

Source: Monetary Authority of Singapore. SGFinDex. https://www.mas.gov.sg/development/fintech/sgfindex.

To enable all these use cases, there are two main uses of open banking APIs: Account information consultation and payment initiation.

Account Information Consultation

Account information consultation uses open banking APIs to capture one or more data points from a customer's bank account. This information could be used to identify subscriptions, in the case of subscription management, or overall financial standing for wealth management. The account information consultation process is as follows:

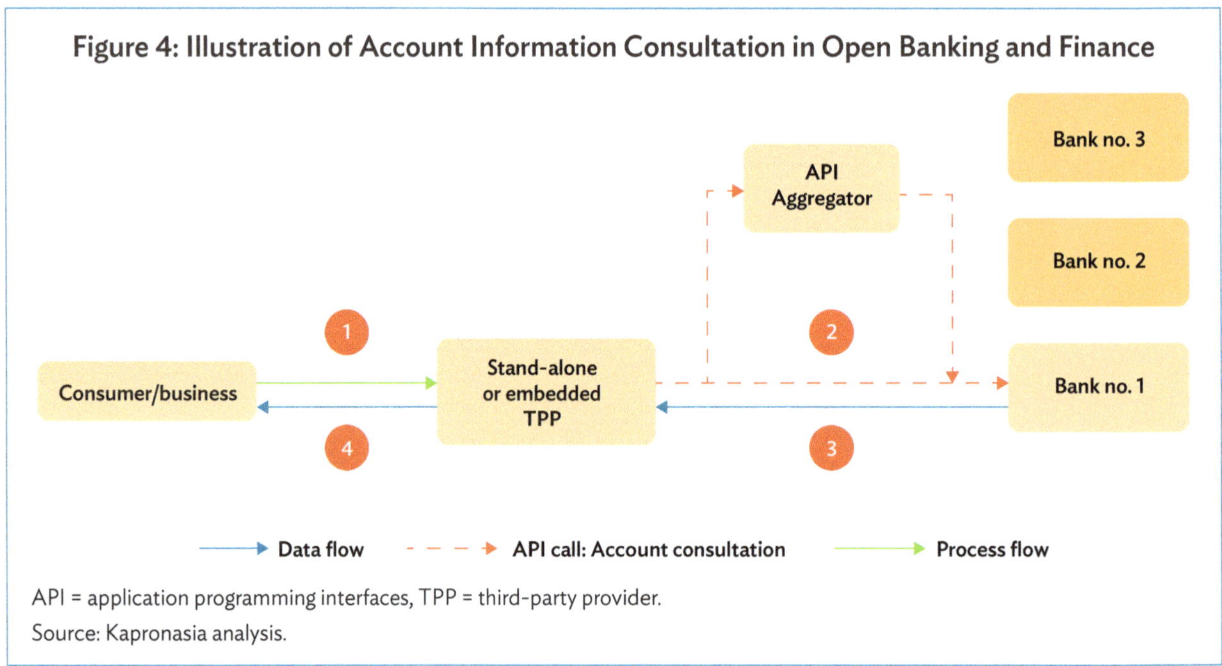

Figure 4: Illustration of Account Information Consultation in Open Banking and Finance

API = application programming interfaces, TPP = third-party provider.
Source: Kapronasia analysis.

(i) **Consumer consent.** The consumer or business grants consent to a licensed third-party provider to access their account data across multiple banks.

(ii) **Data request.** The third-party provider, utilizing open banking APIs, retrieves the account information from various banks where the consumer holds accounts. For this, the third-party provider can directly connect to the individual banks and retrieve information or connect to an API aggregator who already has all the different banking APIs collected.

(iii) **Data aggregation.** Now, the collected data is aggregated by the third-party provider. This data may include account balances, transaction history, and other financial details.

(iv) **Information presentation.** The third-party provider processes this data and presents a unified view of the consumer's financial situation. This may include not just a simple aggregation of account balances but also value-added services such as categorizing transactions, analyzing spending patterns, and providing financial insights.

Using analytical tools, the third-party provider may offer additional services like financial planning assistance, identifying savings opportunities, or even suggesting account products that could optimize the consumer's financial health.

Payment Initiation

Account information consultation only enables "read" access to the account. However, if the consumer wishes to perform financial actions based on the information provided, then they may have to grant read-and-write access. An example of when this is required is in the case of payment initiation, where a customer can use a payment initiation service provider to make payments. This could include transferring funds between a user's accounts (also known as "sweeping"), making bill payments, or setting up regular automatic transfers for things like payroll. A payment initiation service provider can offer open banking as a plugin for mobile apps, platforms, and marketplaces (as well as enabling client merchants).

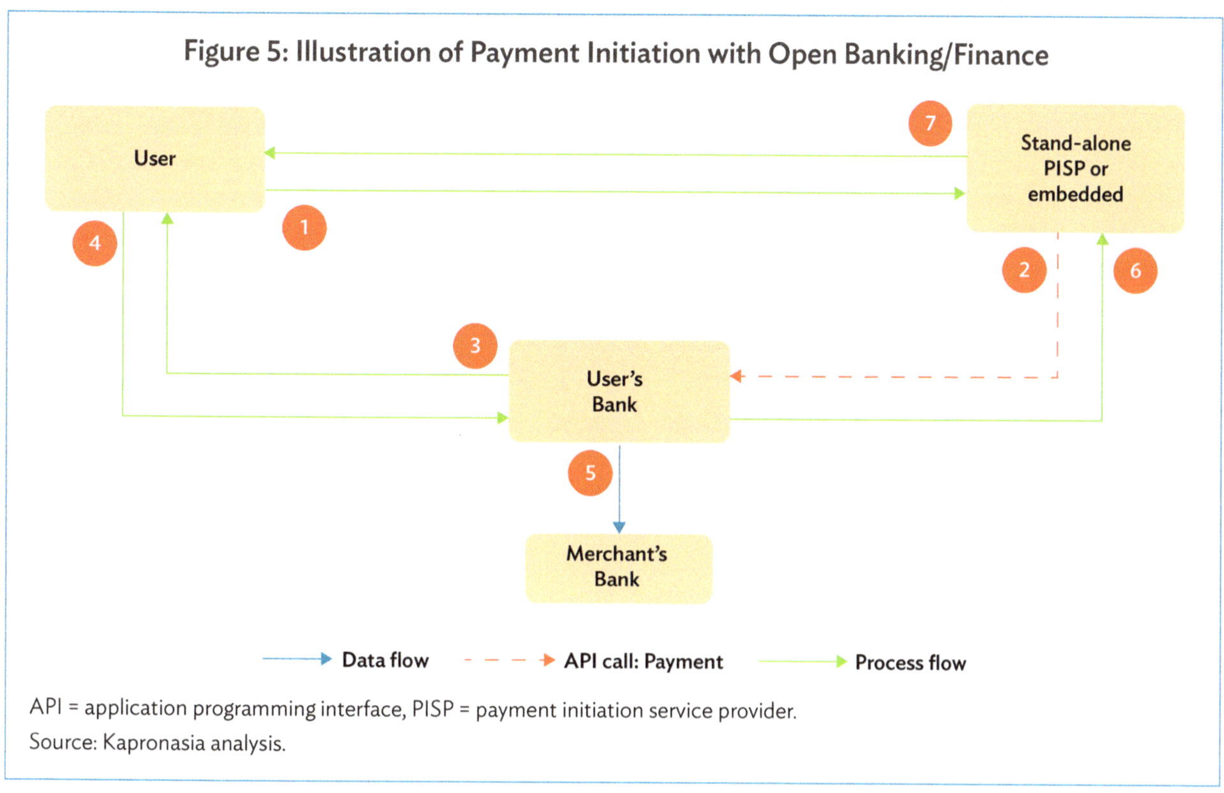

Figure 5: Illustration of Payment Initiation with Open Banking/Finance

API = application programming interface, PISP = payment initiation service provider.
Source: Kapronasia analysis.

The process of payment initiation is typically as follows:

(i)   The user makes a payment request.
(ii)   The payment initiation service provider sends a payment initiation request through open banking APIs to the user or consumer's bank to transfer funds. This could be to another account within the same bank or to an external bank account.
(iii)   The bank processes the payment initiation request and sends a payment-order consent to the user.
(iv)   The user approves or denies the consent.
(v)   The bank executes the payment or declines it.
(vi)   Confirmation is sent by the bank back to the payment initiation service provider.
(vii)   The consumer is then notified that the payment has been successfully initiated and processed.

Throughout this process, all data flows and API calls are secured and operate under the strict consent of the consumer, ensuring privacy and compliance with financial regulations.

The third-party provider (either account information service provider, payment initiation service provider, or both) acts as an intermediary, facilitating both the account information service and payment initiation service and streamlining the consumer's financial activities across multiple banking platforms. In certain cases, the third-party provider may connect into another platform or may be connected to the user directly.

In addition to account information consolidation and payment initiation, APIs can also be used to retrieve non-customer-specific data, which might include product information or specific pricing for a product, such as the exchange rate for a certain currency pair.

Benefits of Open Finance

The benefits of open banking and open finance are similar and extend across the entire financial ecosystem, and can positively impact consumers, businesses, financial institutions, and the economy at large. These benefits underscore the potential of open finance to not only enhance the efficiency and accessibility of financial services but also to spur innovation and inclusive economic growth, as illustrated in Figure 6.

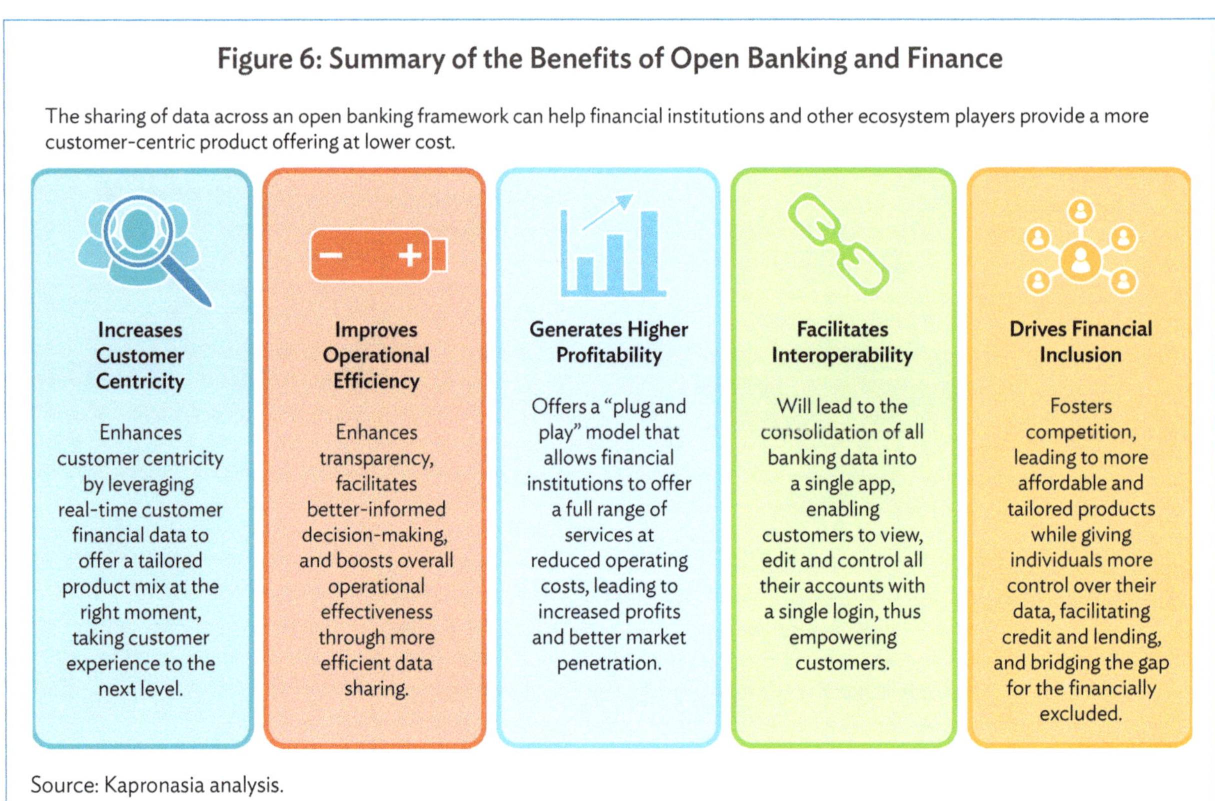

Figure 6: Summary of the Benefits of Open Banking and Finance

The sharing of data across an open banking framework can help financial institutions and other ecosystem players provide a more customer-centric product offering at lower cost.

Source: Kapronasia analysis.

Customer Empowerment

Open finance offers customer empowerment by putting them in control of their financial data. The shift toward data ownership and consent-based data sharing allows individuals to leverage their financial information to access personalized financial products and services. Customers can benefit from improved choice and a more tailored banking experience, with recommendations and advice based on their unique financial situation, leading to better financial decision-making and management.

SMEs and individuals with limited financial transaction history or lack of documentation often face difficulties in fulfilling the stringent KYC requirements of traditional lenders. By leveraging the power of alternative data sources, such as utility bills, rental payments, and mobile money transactions, financial institutions can assess the creditworthiness of these individuals and institutions more accurately in the absence of any documentation, thus offering better access to financial products for entities and individuals traditionally excluded from the credit system due to KYC challenges.

Stimulation of Innovation and Competition

In addition to empowering customers, open banking and open finance can encourage innovation and competition. Many Asian markets lack sufficient competition due to incumbent financial service providers that have little reason to innovate. With bank customer data now available for sharing through APIs, fintech startups and nonfinancial companies can leverage it to develop new, innovative financial products and services. This competition drives down costs, improves service quality, and accelerates digital transformation in the financial sector. The dynamic environment encourages continuous improvement and adaptation, ensuring that the financial services industry remains responsive to consumer needs and technological advancements.

Monetization Opportunities

Open finance provides monetization opportunities for both banks and third-party service providers. Banks can enhance the customer experience, expand their service reach, and potentially generate new revenue streams by offering premium features and functionalities through open banking APIs to third-party platforms. These APIs can be monetized through various pricing models, such as pay-per-use, freemium, tiered, or fixed fees, allowing banks to tailor their approach based on the specific service and data offered.

Third-party providers, on the other hand, can leverage open finance data to develop and offer a broader range of financial products and services, ultimately leading to their growth and success. They can charge customers for services like subscription-based personal finance management tools, convenience fees for streamlining product applications, or commission fees from companies receiving payments facilitated by the third-party providers.

Figure 7: Summary of Monetization Opportunities for Banks and Third-Party Providers

Monetization Opportunities for Banks

Free of charge APIs
Providing such services to customers via third-parties will help banks improve customer experience, increase the penetration of services, and potentially increase customer acquisition for banks.

Premium APIs
Banks can charge third-party platforms for premium APIs, through one of the following pricing models;

- Pay-per-use: No minimum fee, charge per call/per month.
- Free + Premium: Free for basic; more information requires premium pricing.
- Tiered: Tiered pricing for predefined buckets.
- Fixed fee: A fixed/percentage of transaction paid to the API provider.

Monetization Opportunities for TPPs

Free of charge APIs
Third-party platforms can change their customer for add-on services such as personal finance management on a subscription/freemium basis. For product application, TPPs can charge a convenience fee to the customer. In addition, Third party platforms can charge a commission fee to companies to which the payments are made. TPPs can also offer value-added services and charge customers for the same.

Premium APIs
Newer products and premium services can be offered by third-party platforms to their customers, which they can charge for through competitive pricing.

API = application programming interface, TPP = third-party provider.
Source: Kapronasia analysis.

Increased Efficiency and Reduced Costs

By streamlining data sharing and processing, financial institutions can offer faster, more reliable services at a lower cost. This efficiency extends to the customer experience, with simplified processes for accessing financial services and managing finances, which reduces customer churn. Additionally, aggregating financial information from multiple sources in one platform can save consumers time and money, making financial management more convenient and accessible.

Fostering a Collaborative Ecosystem

Open finance encourages collaboration between various stakeholders in the financial ecosystem, including banks, fintech firms, regulatory bodies, and consumers. This collaborative approach facilitates the sharing of insights, best practices, and innovations, contributing to the collective growth and development of the financial services industry. By working together, stakeholders can address challenges, harness opportunities, and drive forward the agenda of financial inclusion and digital transformation.

Enhanced Financial Inclusion

Finally, one of the most promising potential benefits of open finance, and the focus of this paper, is its ability to significantly improve financial inclusion. Open finance can bridge the gap in financial access by facilitating access to a broader range of financial services for underserved and unbanked populations. By integrating various financial products and services, individuals and small businesses previously excluded from the formal financial system can participate more fully in the economy. This inclusivity fosters social equity and economic empowerment, enabling more people to save, invest, and manage financial risks effectively.

The benefits of open finance are multifaceted, and its full potential can only be unlocked if there are robust safeguards to protect consumers, financial institutions, and the broader l market from existing and emerging threats. This necessitates prioritizing data security, ensuring user information is protected from unauthorized access, improper use, and potential breaches; and mitigating other operational and systemic risks.[9]

Risks of Open Banking and Finance

While open banking and open finance present a unique opportunity for the financial industry to make products and services more inclusive, the risks should be considered and accounted for in any open banking or open finance strategy.

It is crucial for regulators, financial institutions, and industry stakeholders to carefully assess and mitigate these risks through robust governance frameworks, consumer protection measures, and collaborative efforts to ensure the sustainable and equitable growth of the open banking and open finance ecosystem.

---

[9]   Organisation for Economic Co-operation and Development (OECD). 2023. Open Finance Policy Considerations. *OECD Business and Finance Policy Papers.* OECD Publishing. https://doi.org/10.1787/19ef3608-en.

Data Privacy and Cybersecurity Concerns

The exchange of sensitive financial data in open banking raises valid concerns about privacy and security, especially for vulnerable populations. For instance, individuals with a limited understanding of data protection measures may fall victim to phishing scams or unauthorized access to their financial information. Without robust safeguards in place, marginalized groups are at a higher risk of identity theft and financial fraud, which can have severe repercussions on their financial stability and well-being.

In addition, as services move online, cybersecurity is a paramount concern in the realm of open banking, given the sensitive nature of financial data and the potential risks associated with its exposure. The interconnected nature of open banking ecosystems introduces new vulnerabilities that can be exploited by malicious actors.

To address these cybersecurity challenges effectively, a proactive approach is essential. This involves implementing robust security measures such as multifactor authentication, encryption of data in transit and at rest, and continuous monitoring of suspicious activities.

Additionally, fostering collaboration among industry stakeholders, sharing threat intelligence, and adhering to global security standards like ISO27032:2012 and NIST cyber security framework are crucial steps toward enhancing the resilience of open banking platforms against cyber threats. By prioritizing cybersecurity best practices and staying vigilant against evolving threats, the financial industry can safeguard customer data, maintain trust, and ensure the success of open banking initiatives.

Ecosystem Risks

The interconnected nature of the open banking/finance ecosystem, with multiple providers accessing and sharing data, creates more potential points of failure for data security.[10] A single bad actor gaining access through lax security practices at one provider could compromise the entire ecosystem, necessitating stringent vetting and enforcement of security protocols across all participants.

Market Inefficiencies

The open banking and finance landscape introduces not only data and ecosystem risks but also business challenges stemming from market inefficiencies. One significant risk is the rapid development and marketing of inappropriate or unsuitable financial services to consumers due to heightened competition and innovation, potentially leading to harmful financial outcomes.

Moreover, certain markets, such as the UK, face the potential for greater inefficiency due to an oversaturation of fintech companies. This oversaturation can result in market fragmentation and increased complexity, making it challenging for consumers to navigate the multitude of options.

Another concern is the potential for unfair competition. While banks are mandated to share their data with third-party providers (as in the UK), other entities, such as big tech firms may not be subject to the same data-sharing obligations, despite possessing vast amounts of financial and nonfinancial information, creating an uneven playing field.

---

[10]   Deloitte. 2017. Open Banking, Open Risk? https://www2.deloitte.com/uk/en/pages/financial-services/articles/open-banking-open-risk.html.

Regulatory Risks

Though open banking and finance regulations are necessary to protect consumers, they cause a burden for the banks as well as the regulators. On one hand, banks face significant costs in complying with regulations and policies related to open banking and open finance, which may strain their resources and hinder innovation. On the other hand, regulators face the challenge of licensing and supervising a growing number of fintech companies operating in open banking/finance, potentially leading to regulatory bottlenecks and oversight challenges.

Challenges of Open Banking and Open Finance

Despite its promise, the open banking and finance ecosystem faces significant challenges across multiple fronts, which can perpetuate existing inequalities and hinder the widespread adoption of open banking initiatives.

Technical Complexities

Developing secure APIs, integrating legacy systems with modern architectures, ensuring data interoperability, and managing large-scale data sharing among multiple parties pose significant technical hurdles. Overcoming these challenges necessitates robust technical expertise, rigorous testing, and adherence to industry standards.

Many financial institutions still rely on legacy systems that were not designed for open data sharing and interoperability. Integrating these dated systems with modern open banking and open finance architectures can be a significant challenge, requiring careful planning, extensive testing, potential system overhauls, and significant investment.

Digital Divide

The digital divide poses a significant challenge in open banking, particularly for underserved or marginalized populations. Access to technology and digital literacy is crucial for individuals to fully engage with open banking services. For example, individuals in rural areas or low-income communities may lack reliable internet access or smartphones, limiting their ability to effectively utilize online banking or fintech platforms. This disparity can further isolate these populations from mainstream financial services, hindering their financial inclusion and exacerbating existing inequalities.

Participants in the open finance ecosystem should ensure that the targeted customer base has sufficient technology and infrastructure access to any financial platforms. Considerations for "fall-back" options like unstructured supplementary service data-enabled services for those individuals or businesses who do not have smartphones and building in offline functionality are two examples of how this might work in practice.

Limited Financial Inclusion

Despite the goal of promoting financial inclusion, open banking may not always reach all segments of the population, particularly the unbanked. For example, individuals without a traditional bank account may struggle to access open banking services that require a linked account for participation. This limitation can perpetuate financial exclusion for marginalized communities, preventing them from fully benefiting from the innovative financial products and services offered through open banking platforms.

Addressing the challenge of limited financial inclusion requires a multifaceted approach to ensure that underserved populations have access to essential financial services.

One potential mitigation strategy involves leveraging digital financial services and innovative technologies to reach individuals traditionally excluded from the banking system. By promoting mobile banking, digital payments, and fintech solutions, financial institutions can extend their services to remote or underserved areas, providing a convenient and affordable means for individuals to access banking services.

Additionally, fostering partnerships between financial institutions, government agencies, and community organizations can help create tailored financial products and services that cater to the specific needs of marginalized populations.

Inadequate Financial Education

A lack of financial education presents a significant barrier for underserved populations looking to engage with open banking. For instance, individuals with limited financial literacy may struggle to understand the risks and benefits associated with sharing their financial data through open banking channels. Without access to proper guidance and resources, these individuals may make uninformed decisions that could compromise their financial security and well-being, highlighting the importance of tailored financial education programs to empower marginalized communities in navigating open banking services effectively.

Governments, regulators, industry associations, financial institutions, and third-party providers should focus on creating programs and initiatives for individuals and businesses to help them better understand the risks and benefits associated with the financial products and services offered using open banking and open finance principles.

Enabling Pillars of Open Banking and Open Finance

The successful realization of open finance hinges on several foundational pillars that together create a robust ecosystem capable of fostering innovation, ensuring security, and promoting inclusivity. These pillars—regulatory support, technological infrastructure, consumer consent and trust, and collaboration among stakeholders—serve as the cornerstones for open finance.

Regulatory Support

Regulatory frameworks play a pivotal role in the open finance ecosystem, providing the necessary guidelines and protections to ensure data sharing benefits all parties involved. Effective regulation balances the need for innovation with the imperative of safeguarding consumer rights and privacy.

Regulatory frameworks help establish a foundation for open finance by setting clear and consistent standards, particularly for APIs. Regulators achieve this through defining data formats and functionalities, fostering collaboration between financial institutions and third-party providers to develop these standards, and prioritizing data security and consumer privacy within the APIs. For example, the UK's Open Banking Implementation Entity successfully developed the Open Banking Standard through collaboration, which has significantly eased integration for third-party providers and fueled innovation in the financial sector.[11] Standardized open finance APIs lead to increased adoption by lowering barriers to entry for third-party providers, reducing development costs, and ultimately enhancing the user experience by enabling seamless interaction with various financial services.

Moreover, regulatory support extends beyond merely establishing rules; it encompasses active engagement with industry to adapt regulations as the financial landscape evolves. This dynamic regulatory approach is crucial for addressing emerging challenges and leveraging new opportunities in the fast-paced world of financial technology.

Technological Infrastructure

The backbone of open finance is its technological infrastructure, which enables the secure and efficient exchange of data across different platforms and providers. APIs are at the heart of this infrastructure, allowing seamless interoperability between financial institutions, third-party providers, and consumers. These technologies facilitate data sharing and ensure such exchanges are conducted securely, protecting sensitive financial information against unauthorized access and breaches. Moreover, advancements in blockchain, AI, and cloud computing enhance the open finance ecosystem, offering solutions for data storage, analysis, and privacy that were unimaginable a few decades ago. Investing in robust technological infrastructure is essential for the scalability and sustainability of open finance, enabling the ecosystem to support a growing number of services and users.

Consumer Consent and Trust

At the core of open finance is the principle of consumer consent, which empowers individuals with control over their financial data. This consent-based model is fundamental for building trust between consumers and financial service providers. Trust is the currency of open finance; without it, the willingness of consumers to share their data and engage with new financial services diminishes. Therefore, establishing explicit, transparent data sharing and handling practices is crucial. This also includes the right for consumers to withdraw consent and have their data deleted. Consumers must be assured of their data's security and be informed of how and why it is used. This transparency fosters trust and encourages consumers' active participation in the open finance ecosystem, driving its growth and diversity.

Collaboration Among Stakeholders

Open finance thrives on collaborating with various stakeholders, including financial institutions, fintech companies, regulatory bodies, and consumers. This collaborative effort is essential for creating a cohesive and interoperable financial ecosystem that benefits all parties.

Financial institutions bring a wealth of experience, data, and resources, while fintech companies offer innovation and agility. Regulatory bodies provide the framework for these collaborations to flourish, ensuring consumer interests are protected. Meanwhile, consumers, with their consent and participation, drive demand for personalized and accessible financial services.

---

[11]   Open Banking Limited. About Open Banking Limited. https://www.openbanking.org.uk/about-us/#:~:text=Open%20Banking%20Limited%20(OBL)%20%E2%80%93,Banking%20Standard%20and%20industry%20guidelines.

While open finance thrives on stakeholder collaboration, achieving full participation poses challenges. Many major financial institutions currently do not embrace open finance, fearing a loss of competitive edge if required to share data and access. Though fintech companies promote innovation and consumers want personalized financial services, banks resist opening systems that are seen as proprietary advantages. This hesitancy slows industry transformation. This can be addressed by mandating open finance and banking through regulation, as implemented in Europe and the UK. This could accelerate progress but risks alienating the financial sector further. Ultimately, stakeholders must align on a shared vision for an interoperable financial ecosystem benefiting all parties. Financial institutions need persuading that open finance, done equitably, expands markets without forfeiting leadership. The synergy between these stakeholders fosters continuous innovation and improvement, pushing the boundaries of what is possible in financial services.

III. The Promise of Open Finance

While open banking does not directly increase the number of people with bank accounts, it can play a crucial role in improving the financial health and landscape of the underbanked population. These are individuals or businesses that have bank accounts but are not adequately served by traditional financial institutions. By using open banking data, new and improved financial products and services can be customized to better meet their needs.

In developed economies such as Singapore, Japan, and Australia, while financial inclusion rates are high, usually in the region of 97%–99%, there are still pockets of underserved or vulnerable populations. Open banking could improve financial inclusion, health, and resilience and drive value for those on the margins of financial inclusion (with no account or only a basic account) by helping them control their finances, obtain better deals, and manage debt.[12] In developed markets like Singapore, this might also include SMEs, which tend to be overlooked by traditional banks even in heavily banked countries.

In developing economies, where large parts of the population have limited access to banking services, the rapid increase in digital data, driven by improvements in digital technology and access (especially the growing ownership of smartphones), presents an unparalleled opportunity. If open banking systems in these economies were expanded to include data from other financial service providers (open finance), such as mobile money accounts, as well as nonfinancial sectors like utilities and telecommunications (open data), it could significantly improve financial inclusion in reach, depth, and usefulness. Transactional data, for example, can enhance customer segmentation and risk assessment and develop gender targeted solutions, fostering more effective underwriting, competitive pricing, and product customization to individual needs. Transactional data becomes a lifeline for those lacking traditional credit histories, offering them access to previously out-of-reach credit facilities.

Beyond credit, the utility of data in open finance extends to a broader spectrum of financial services, including embedded insurance and personal financial management. These services leverage data to help providers understand customer behavior better, design responsive products, and facilitate smoother customer experiences, contributing to a more inclusive financial landscape.

This broader data integration is essential for opening up financial services and account access to those outside the financial system. Thus, for open banking regimes to effectively support financial inclusion and offer more valuable services to the unbanked and the underbanked, they must adopt a comprehensive approach to data exchange beyond just banking data to include a wide array of sectors.

---

[12]   Open Banking Limited, Faith Reynolds & Mark Chidley. 2019. Consumer Priorities for Open Banking.

However, the realization of open finance's full potential is not without challenges. Data accessibility remains a significant hurdle, with data often held in silos and large incumbent players dominating the data landscape. The development of open finance ecosystems promises to address these challenges by reducing information asymmetry, fostering a more competitive and innovative market, and ultimately driving the expansion and deepening of financial inclusion.

It is worth reviewing a few open finance use cases to illustrate some of the opportunities it presents for advancing financial inclusion.

Alternative Credit Scores for Lending

One of the key challenges in underbanked populations is the lack of financial transactional data. Individuals or businesses that have previously not interacted much with the traditional financial system will be "thin-file" insofar as they have very little credit history. Because of this, it becomes difficult for traditional financial institutions to lend to these customers cost-effectively.

Alternative credit scoring involves using nontraditional data sources, beyond standard credit bureau reports, to assess the creditworthiness of an individual or business. These data can include utility bill payments, mobile money transactions, e-commerce activity, social media data, and other digital footprints.

Lenders can access a more comprehensive view of a borrower's financial behavior and payment patterns by leveraging open finance frameworks that enable secure data sharing across platforms. Advanced analytics and machine learning models are then applied to this alternative data to generate credit scores that reflect the borrower's true risk profile.

For individuals without credit histories, alternative credit scores can unlock access to loans, credit cards, and other financial products that were previously out of reach. This can subsequently empower them to invest in things like education and business opportunities, or to meet other financial needs, fostering economic growth and social mobility.

SMEs, which also often struggle to obtain financing due to limited credit histories or inadequate collateral, can also benefit significantly from alternative credit scoring. Lenders can better assess SMEs' creditworthiness and extend tailored financing solutions by considering their digital footprints, such as sales data, vendor payments, and cash flow patterns.

It is worth highlighting that in the case of alternative data, not all of the information is coming from financial institutions but may come from other providers, which may include digital wallets, apps, and other digital platforms. However, the third-party provider or fintech would likely still incorporate data from traditional service providers leveraging open banking and open finance. Data from telecommunications companies or other platforms would be considered open data.

Case Study

FinScore is an award-winning alternative credit scoring company from the Philippines powered by telecommunications data and advanced analytics.

A multinational online loan provider new to the Philippines wanted to offer quick credit solutions to the underbanked population. The challenge was assessing creditworthiness without traditional credit data.[13] FinScore helped build credit scores from mobile network data using advanced algorithms targeting the underbanked segment. Additionally, the score could be retrieved quickly via an API, allowing for easy integration within just 2 days. The "telco score" integrated seamlessly, and within a week, FinScore had delivered over 1,000 scores to the client. This innovative use of alternative data gave the company a unique advantage in assessing the underbanked market. Overall, FinScore's Telco Score empowered the loan provider to reach a new customer base, promoting financial inclusion and economic opportunity in the Philippines.

Embedded Lending

Embedded lending is the integration of lending services into nonfinancial companies' platforms to provide accessible and personalized credit solutions for both consumers and SMEs, ultimately creating a more seamless lending experience. Data obtained through open finance can help provide credit scoring and a link back to the traditional financial services provider that might be underwriting the lending.

The potential is enormous for financial inclusion within embedded lending. By leveraging alternative credit assessment methods and streamlining the application process, embedded lending ensures that individuals who may have been previously excluded from traditional banking systems now have access to much-needed credit.

Moreover, embedded lending facilitates credit provision to a wider base of individuals in a more convenient and accessible way. This approach also helps address the supply and demand mismatch for working capital and financing for SMEs, particularly in the context of marketplace and accounting platforms where there is a rich data set that can be leveraged. By assisting SMEs with their short-term cash flow needs, embedded lending on these platforms enables SMEs to purchase more inventory, invest in their growth, and seize opportunities.

Case Study

In 2022, Xero, a New Zealand-based accounting software as a service provider, partnered with the Development Bank of Singapore (DBS), a Singaporean-based bank, to digitalize SME lending in Singapore and Hong Kong, China. This collaboration aimed to simplify loan applications and improve access to working capital for SMEs. DBS and Xero began their partnership in 2017 with a bank feed integration to give SMEs greater visibility and control over their finances with automatic bank updates.

By opting into direct bank feeds, Singapore and Hong Kong, China SMEs could securely share transactional records with DBS. This helped the bank better understand their cash flow and personalize lending options. Since 2020, DBS has approved over 14,000 collateral-free loans, with 90% benefiting micro and small enterprises, contributing S$6.4 billion to Singapore's economy.[14]

---

13 FinScore. 2022. Unique Insight for the Underbanked Segment: A FinScore Case Study. https://www.finscore.ph/wp-content/uploads/2022/07/Unique-Insight-for-the-Underbanked-Segment.pdf.

14 Developmental Bank of Singapore. 2022. DBS and Xero Make it Easier for SMEs to Access Working Capital with Hyper-Personalised Lending Solutions. Press Release. 4 May. https://www.dbs.com/NewsPrinter.page?newsId=l2aaqm7v&locale=en.

Embedded Insurance

Embedded insurance is a model that seamlessly integrates insurance solutions into the customer journey through non-insurance channels. This approach enables the provision of insurance as a native feature, conveniently embedded either at the point of sale or within the product itself, thereby weaving insurance into the fabric of customers' daily lives and work. The aim is to offer affordable, relevant, and customized insurance precisely when customers need it most, enhancing their experience and providing peace of mind.

From the perspective of insurance companies, embedded insurance opens up a new distribution channel that promises to acquire new clients en masse at a considerably lower cost without incurring extra risks. This model allows insurers to tap into a wealth of customer data, including financial, life event, behavioral, and location information, through the use of APIs. Access to such rich datasets enables insurers to make more accurate underwriting and actuarial decisions, tailoring their offerings to meet the specific needs and circumstances of their customers.

Furthermore, the leverage of alternative data sources through open banking significantly enhances the potential of embedded insurance. Alternative data facilitates a more nuanced understanding of customers, offering insights into previously untapped or under-served market segments. By analyzing a broader range of data, insurers can identify new opportunities within market segments that were previously considered too risky or not commercially viable. This approach not only expands the market reach of insurers but also contributes to a more inclusive insurance ecosystem, where a wider array of individuals and businesses can benefit from tailored, risk-appropriate protection solutions.

In addition to traditional products, new offerings, such as pricing for climate risks are expected to shift to an embedded model. By making climate risk protection more accessible and visible at critical touchpoints, embedded insurance has the potential to bridge the "protection gap" for climate-related risks. However, challenges remain for embedded climate-risk insurance, such as insufficient data granularity and difficulty in using appropriate climate modeling tools.

Case Study

PasarPolis, a digital insurance company from Indonesia, played a pivotal role in helping more Indonesians protect against risk through the innovative application of embedded insurance. At its inception, insurance penetration in Indonesia stood below 3%, largely due to low insurance literacy and reluctance among individuals, particularly low-income families, to purchase policies.

Through technology, PasarPolis offered low-priced microinsurance solutions tailored to various situations, including accidents and broken gadgets. The company developed an embedded system that allowed it to distribute insurance through partner channels such as ride-hailing apps, e-commerce platforms, fintech companies, and travel platforms. Leveraging the ideas behind open finance, the platforms acted as distribution channels and leveraged APIs to pull product and policy information from PasarPolis.

The partner insurance model involved working with offline agents, like mom-and-pop shop owners, to facilitate insurance purchases on their digital platform. As of 2019, the company had issued 650 million policies in the three countries where it operates, namely Indonesia, Thailand, and Viet Nam. Of these, 90% of the policies were for first-time insurance buyers, and 40% of policy holders worked in the informal sector.[15]

---

[15]   PasarPolis. 2020. Aiming to Boost Insurance Penetration, PasarPolis Develops Agency Applications. https://pasarpolis.io/news/bertujuan-genjot-penetrasi-asuransi-pasarpolis-kembangkan-aplikasi-keagenan.

Open Banking Payments

Open banking-enabled payments use open banking APIs to initiate account-to-account transactions that are simple, fast, and low-cost, streamlining the process of moving funds from one account to another without the need for traditional payment intermediaries.

Whether it is for single payments, scheduled payments, bulk transfers, or variable amounts, these transactions are initiated directly from the payer's account provider at the behest of the payer. Once initiated, the payer's payment service provider efficiently moves the funds to credit the payee's account, thereby simplifying transactions across different institutions.

Open banking payments can play a pivotal role in the realm of embedded payments, offering substantial benefits that streamline and enhance the consumer experience across various platforms. By integrating open banking payments into embedded payment systems, businesses can offer their customers seamless, frictionless payment options directly within their service or purchasing journey, eliminating the need for traditional payment intermediaries.

This integration not only expedites the payment process, allowing instant transactions and immediate access to goods or services, but also significantly reduces transaction costs, due to the elimination of intermediary fees associated with traditional payment methods like credit cards, for example. In the cards ecosystem, intermediaries such as payment processors, acquirers, and networks charge fees for facilitating transactions, which can be significant.

Furthermore, the inherent security features of open banking payments stem from the direct bank-to-bank transfer mechanism, which eliminates the need to share sensitive financial information with third parties. This approach reduces the risk of data breaches and fraud, as sensitive information is not exposed to multiple entities in the transaction chain. Additionally, open banking typically leverages robust authentication protocols, such as two-factor authentication and secure APIs, ensuring that only authorized parties can initiate and complete transactions.

Before the advent of open banking, businesses often faced challenges with cash flow and liquidity due to the delayed settlement of transactions through traditional payment methods. Credit card settlements, for instance, can take several days to reflect in a merchant's account, leading to temporary cash flow constraints. In addition, reconciling transactions could be challenging due to a lack of integration between systems.

With Open Banking, the direct bank-to-bank transfer mechanism facilitates near-instant settlements, improving cash flow and liquidity for businesses. Furthermore, since the transactions are initiated and authorized directly by the customer's bank, the risk of chargebacks is much lower.

The risk of fraud is also lower. Transactions are initiated by the customer, and open banking enables businesses to access more detailed customer data, which can help them identify potential fraud more quickly.

Case Study

Volume, a UK-based fintech founded in 2021 with the mission to optimize online checkout experiences, embarked on a strategic partnership with Yapily, another UK fintech specializing in open banking solutions.[16]

---

[16]   Yapily. 2022. Case Study: How Yapily and Volume Are Killing Hidden Fees for Businesses and Consumers. https://www.yapily.com/blog/open-banking-case-study-volume.

Their collaboration aimed to address the challenge of costly hidden fees in electronic transactions, which have long burdened both businesses and consumers.

Merchants routinely lose 2% to 8% of every sale to the fees imposed by card, e-wallet, and buy-now-pay later facilitators (known as BNPL). These expenses, significant as they are, inevitably trickle down to consumers, manifesting as inflated prices for goods and services.

To counter this, Volume leveraged its partnership with Yapily to spearhead a more equitable financial ecosystem. By employing Yapily's robust open banking platform, Volume was able to introduce Transparent Checkout, a revolutionary online payment solution. This system seamlessly directs shoppers to their banking app for secure biometric authentication, facilitating direct, instant bank-to-bank payments to merchants. This process not only bypasses traditional payment intermediaries but also significantly diminishes the cost of transactions.

The impact of this innovation has been profound. Merchants now enjoy a transaction process with increased settlement speed and devoid of the hidden fees that once eroded their profits. Perhaps most notably, the ease and efficiency of the transparent checkout system have led to a surge in checkout conversion rates.

Smart Onboarding

Smart onboarding significantly improves the customer journey by speeding up the account opening process. In open banking, third-party providers, with explicit customer consent, can access and consolidate account and transaction information from the user's banking institutions. This information is then used to autofill applications to streamline the onboarding process.

Leveraging open banking, banks and fintechs are able to more quickly and accurately onboard individuals and businesses by leveraging pre-existing identification and account information. Prior to open banking, the KYC process typically required each financial institution to verify and validate a customer's identity and documentation independently, often leading to redundant efforts and delays. However, with open banking, established guidelines and regulations allow financial institutions to securely share and rely on KYC information already collected by other regulated entities, subject to customer consent.

This increased efficiency improves the user experience and can positively impact conversion rates. When combined with payment initiation consent and APIs, accounts can be funded quickly, increasing the speed with which users can obtain new financial products and services.

Regulatory frameworks provide guidelines and standards for secure data sharing, ensuring that KYC information is shared through secure APIs and with appropriate customer consent. These regulations also establish liability models and guidelines for financial institutions to follow when relying on KYC information from other regulated entities. This ensures a robust and trustworthy system for customer onboarding and account opening.

Smart onboarding makes it easier for SMEs to access essential financial services such as business accounts, loans, and payment solutions, empowering them to manage their finances effectively and grow their businesses. Similarly, individuals benefit from simplified account opening procedures, enabling them to easily access banking services and credit products tailored to their needs.

Case Study

In 2019, Swedish investment bank Avanza collaborated with Tink, an open banking platform, to enhance the customer onboarding experience.[17]

Avanza experienced high abandonment rates during the account opening process, largely due to the cumbersome requirement that customers manually fill out online application forms.

To tackle this issue, Avanza utilized Tink's advanced aggregation technology. This integration allowed for the automatic retrieval of data from customers' existing bank accounts, which was then used to pre-fill personal details in Avanza's application forms. This streamlined the process of transferring funds from a customer's other bank accounts to Avanza, simplifying the process of switching and consolidating savings.

Implementing Tink's technology transformed the customer experience, making it more seamless and user-friendly. Thanks to the elimination of manual data entry, Avanza witnessed a dramatic enhancement in its onboarding flows. Most notably, the collaboration led to a 150% increase in conversion rates, indicating a significant improvement in customer satisfaction and engagement.

Box 3: Open Finance for Sustainable Consumption and Climate Change

The use case of open finance for sustainable consumption and climate change represents a forward-thinking application of financial technology that aligns financial decision-making with environmental stewardship. By harnessing the power of open finance, innovative platforms can provide users with the tools to understand and mitigate their environmental impact through their everyday financial activities.

Such platforms analyze transaction data to calculate the carbon footprint of purchases, offering users a tangible connection between their spending habits and their environmental impact. This can range from the carbon intensity of their grocery shopping to the broader implications of their travel and energy consumption patterns. By integrating these insights directly into financial applications, users can receive real-time feedback on how their choices contribute to their carbon footprint, alongside suggestions for more sustainable alternatives.

Moreover, these platforms often go beyond mere tracking and analysis to actively encourage and facilitate more environmentally friendly consumption choices. This could involve recommending eco-friendly products and services, offering incentives for sustainable purchases, or even providing options to offset carbon emissions directly through the app. For instance, a user might be prompted to invest in renewable energy projects or participate in reforestation efforts to counterbalance their carbon footprint.

The broader implication of this open finance use case is the potential for systemic change toward sustainability in the consumer economy. By making environmental impact a visible and actionable aspect of financial decision-making, these platforms can drive a shift in consumer behavior toward more sustainable practices. Furthermore, they provide businesses with insights into consumer preferences for sustainability, potentially influencing product development and corporate sustainability strategies.

continued on next page

---

[17]   Tink. 2019. Tink and Avanza Collaborates to Improve Customer Experience. https://tink.com/press/tink-avanza-partnership/.

Box 3 *continued*

One notable example of a company that has leveraged open finance to promote sustainable consumption and climate change initiatives is Doconomy. Based in Sweden, Doconomy provides a mobile banking service that tracks carbon dioxide emissions associated with purchases, enabling users to understand and manage their carbon footprint through their spending.

Doconomy's service uses transaction data to calculate the carbon impact of each purchase, offering users insights into the environmental cost of their consumption habits. The platform also encourages users to offset their carbon footprint by investing in various climate projects. Furthermore, Doconomy offers a credit card made from bio-sourced materials, emphasizing its commitment to sustainability not just in its services but also in its physical products.

This innovative use of open finance technology exemplifies how financial services can intersect with environmental sustainability, empowering consumers to make more informed choices and contribute to the fight against climate change.

Source: Doconomy. The Doconomy Platform. https://www.doconomy.com/.

IV. The State of Open Finance in Asia and the Pacific

Open banking has revolutionized the financial industry in recent years. Globally, the open banking market, consisting of sales of open banking services by entities (organizations, sole traders, and partnerships), is expected to grow from $15.13 billion in 2021 to $123.70 billion by 2031, growing at a compound annual growth rate of 23.4% from 2021 to 2031.[18] As of 2020, 24.7 million individuals worldwide used open banking services, which is forecast to reach 132.2 million by 2024.[19]

The number of open banking API calls—102 billion in 2023—is expected to increase to 580 billion in 2027. During the same period, the value of open banking transactions is expected to grow sharply as well and reach $330 billion in 2027.[20]

Figure 8 provides a snapshot of the thriving fintech landscape in the Asia and Pacific region as of 2024.

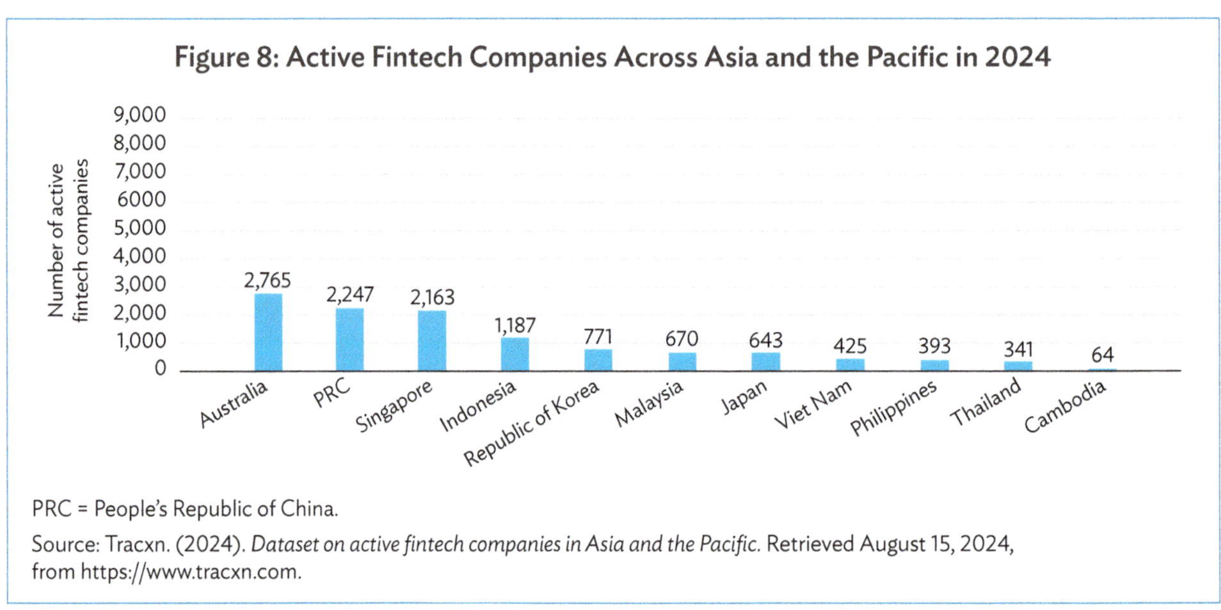

PRC = People's Republic of China.

Source: Tracxn. (2024). *Dataset on active fintech companies in Asia and the Pacific.* Retrieved August 15, 2024, from https://www.tracxn.com.

[18] The Business Research Company. 2022. Open Banking Global Market Report 2022. https://www.thebusinessresearchcompany.com/report/open-banking-global-market-report; Allied Market Research. 2022. Open Banking Market. https://www.alliedmarketresearch.com/open-banking-market.

[19] Statista. 2021. Number of Open Banking Users Worldwide in 2020 with Forecasts from 2021 to 2024, by region (in millions). https://www.statista.com/statistics/1228771/open-banking-users-worldwide/.

[20] Statista. 2023. Number of Open Banking Application Programming Interface (API) Calls in 2023, with a Forecast for 2027 (in billions). https://www.statista.com/statistics/1389414/number-of-open-banking-api-calls-worldwide/.

Market-Driven Versus Regulator-Mandated Open Finance

As open banking and open finance have developed in Asia and the Pacific, a wide range of approaches has emerged, reflecting the region's diverse economic landscapes, regulatory philosophies, and stages of financial technology adoption. This evolution of approaches can be roughly categorized based on the driving forces behind each: market-driven efforts versus regulatory mandates.

(i)   Regulator-mandated approaches are those where there is a regulatory requirement for banks to open their data to third-party providers when customers give consent. Example: Australia. This is similar to the UK's open banking and finance journey.

(ii)   Market-driven approaches do not require banks to share data with third-party providers, but initiatives are largely driven by market forces, including consumer demand, fintech innovation, and competitive pressures among financial institutions. Examples: Kenya, Malaysia, Singapore, Thailand, United States, Viet Nam.

While open banking is mainly market-driven in Asia and the Pacific, with few regulators mandating it, most regulators are encouraging its adoption and actively seeking to steer its direction. Many jurisdictions, such as Singapore, have issued open banking frameworks and/or API standards for the financial sector. Others, such as Hong Kong, China; and the Philippines, have adopted an "opt-in" approach to open banking/finance. Participating institutions in these jurisdictions that have opted-in are obligated to implement agreed-upon regulator-set standards and open their data to third parties, whereas institutions that are not participating are not required to do so.

Open banking and open finance initiatives have been gaining momentum in Central and West Asia, with Kazakhstan and Georgia emerging as pioneers in the region. Kazakhstan has set an ambitious open API-driven strategy to modernize its financial sector by 2025, following a successful pilot project in late 2023.[21] The National Bank of Kazakhstan and the National Payment Corporation of Kazakhstan have developed an open API platform, established standards, and implemented a centralized customer consent management system.[22] Kazakhstan's road map for 2024 includes expanding bank participation, developing business use cases, and implementing an open API technology sandbox.

The open API and open finance initiative in Georgia, initiated by the National Bank and Banking Association of Georgia since 2020, mirrors the European PSD2 directive and the Berlin Group standards.[23] It has been successful, with major banks like TBC and FINCA Bank leading the way in developing compliant open APIs. This has spurred the creation of innovative financial products and services, contributing to the digital transformation of the country's financial sector.

---

[21]   Open Banking Excellence. 2024. Kazakhstan Sets Open API-Driven Strategy Towards 2025 Goal. https://www.openbankingexcellence.org/blog/kazakhstan-sets-open-api-driven-strategy-towards-2025-goal/.

[22]   National Bank of Kazakhstan. 2024. Open API и [and] Open Banking: Report on the result of the pilot project. https://nationalbank.kz/file/download/97963.

[23]   Openbankproject. FINCA Bank Georgia Delivers Compliant API Platform Using Open Bank Project. https://www.openbankproject.com/case-study/finca-bank-georgia-berlin-group-compliance/.

In contrast, the Pacific countries have seen slower progress in open banking and open finance initiatives, perhaps due to geographical challenges, regulatory complexities, economic constraints, and limited technological infrastructure.

A selection of Asia and the Pacific economies' approaches to open finance are highlighted below.

Market-Driven Jurisdictions

Singapore

Singapore has adopted a proactive approach to open banking, spearheaded by the Monetary Authority of Singapore (MAS), which has played an essential role in the country's open banking process. In 2016, The Association of Banks in Singapore, in consultation with the MAS, published the *Finance-as-a-Service API Playbook*, providing comprehensive guidelines on API governance, implementation, use cases, and over 400 recommended APIs for banks.[24] This playbook, which contains information on common and useful APIs, forward-looking technical and information security standards, and industry-relevant corporate data policy and governance, marked the beginning of the open banking/finance regime in Singapore.

Following this, in 2018, MAS, in collaboration with the International Finance Corporation and the Association of Southeast Asian Nations (ASEAN) Bankers' Association, launched the API Exchange, the world's first cross-border, open-architecture platform.[25] The exchange is a collaborative platform for fintechs and financial institutions to innovate and develop/test new products using open APIs.

MAS implemented the Singapore Financial Data Exchange (SGFinDex) in 2020 to further drive adoption, enabling individuals to aggregate their financial data across banks and government agencies.[26] Most recently, the launch of the Singapore Trade Data Exchange (SGTraDex), a digital utility that connects supply chain partners through a common data infrastructure leveraging APIs, showcases Singapore's continued efforts in propelling open finance. While not mandatory, MAS has provided a robust framework and infrastructure to facilitate its open banking/finance adoption.

All of these APIs, and others, are tracked in the Financial Industry API Register run by MAS to provide a directory of open APIs offered by financial institutions in the country.

Malaysia

Malaysia has also taken a market-driven approach to open banking, with regulatory support from Bank Negara Malaysia. In 2019, the central bank published a policy document titled Publishing Open Data using open API, outlining standards that financial institutions intending to publish open data APIs should follow.[27] However, banks are not obligated to share their data, and incumbents see little incentive to open their data troves to third parties. Because of this, the initial adoption of open banking in the country has been low.

---

[24]   The Association of Banks in Singapore. 2016. The Association of Banks in Singapore Issues Finance-As-A-Service: API Playbook. Media Release. 16 November. https://abs.org.sg/docs/library/mediarelease_20161116.pdf.

[25]   Monetary Authority of Singapore. 2018. World's First Cross-Border, Open-Architecture Platform to Improve Financial Inclusion. Media Release. 18 September. https://www.mas.gov.sg/news/media-releases/2018/worlds-first-cross-border-open-architecture-platform-to-improve-financial-inclusion.

[26]   The Asian Banker. 2020. Singapore Financial Data Exchange (SGFinDex) Launched. https://www.theasianbanker.com/press-releases/singapore-financial-data-exchange-(sgfindex)-launched.

[27]   V. Fong, 2018. Why BNM's Open API Initiative Could Bring Malaysia's Fintech into a New Era. Fintech Malaysia. 19 September. https://fintechnews.my/18462/regtech-fintech-regulation-malaysia/bnm-open-api-open-banking/.

The banks offering open APIs have typically provided static product information rather than dynamic customer data. The issuance of five digital bank licenses in 2022, focused on financial inclusion, could potentially accelerate Bank Negara Malaysia's development of open banking frameworks.[28] Additionally, enablers like a national digital identity are being developed to facilitate the secure data sharing required for open banking. While progress has been slower, Malaysia seems to recognize the importance of open banking and is progressively establishing policies and infrastructure to drive adoption within its banking sector.

Republic of Korea

The evolution of open banking in the Republic of Korea has been marked by a strategic blend of market-driven initiatives and public goods, spearheaded by the Financial Services Commission, the country's top financial regulator. However, there is no formal or compulsory open banking regime in the country.

The Republic of Korea currently supports its open banking initiatives with two infrastructure systems: a foundational open banking service initiated in December 2019, which plays a pivotal role in the country's fintech payment infrastructure, and the API-driven MyData service launched in January 2022, acting as a government-endorsed central point for consumers to manage their data within the open banking ecosystem.

The Financial Services Commission has recently introduced initiatives to expand the scope and enhance the usability of open banking. The first of these initiatives aims to broaden the range of accessible data through open banking, encompassing personal and commercial accounts. This enhancement will enable third-party users of open banking to conduct real-time, simultaneous checks across multiple accounts. Specifically, the inclusion of commercial account information is intended to empower financial service providers to offer more tailored fund management solutions to their business clients.

The Financial Services Commission's second initiative focuses on extending open banking services to offline channels, such as physical bank branches. This move is intended to allow account holders to access services like account checks and fund transfers at any bank or branch location.

Viet Nam

Viet Nam is taking a cautious yet proactive approach toward adopting open banking. Although the country lacks a comprehensive legal framework for open banking as of May 2024, several banks have started building the necessary infrastructure and partnerships.

Orient Commercial Joint Stock Bank launched its API portal platform in late 2019, offering over 30 APIs to allow partners to integrate with their systems and create a wider financial ecosystem. VietinBank has introduced the VietinBank iConnect platform with over 127 APIs, collaborating with 73 partners. Bank for Investment and Development of Vietnam has completed a payment portal to connect with nearly 2,000 retail service providers and payment intermediaries.[29]

---

[28] *Business Today.* 2022. Breaking: Bank Negara Awards Digital Bank License To 5 Successful Applicants. 29 April. https://www.businesstoday .com.my/2022/04/29/breaking-bank-negara-awards-digital-bank-license-to-5-succesful-applicants/.

[29] Daututaichinh. 2024. Vietnamese Banks Gear Up for Open Banking. 12 January. https://dttc.sggp.org.vn/vietnamese-banks-gear-up-for -open-banking-post111114.html.

As Viet Nam lacks a dedicated legal framework for open banking, banks have proceeded cautiously while awaiting clear regulations, as open APIs are currently developed individually by each bank without common standards or interoperability. There are also concerns about risks related to privacy, data security, and accountability when enabling third-party access to banking systems through APIs.

While the government's focus on digital transformation and initiatives like eKYC for bank account opening and the Mobile Money program are laying the groundwork for a more connected financial ecosystem, a comprehensive regulatory framework is needed to address issues like criteria for API access, licensing, and responsibilities of banks and third-party providers. The State Bank of Vietnam, the central bank, is working on regulations on open banking and finance.

Regulator-Mandated Jurisdictions

Australia

Australia stands out as one of the few markets in Asia and the Pacific that has taken an unambiguously regulator-led approach to open banking. The Government of Australia enacted the Consumer Data Rights legislation, which came into effect in July 2020, making it mandatory for financial institutions across the country to share customer data through secure open banking APIs. However, the Consumer Data Rights has a broader scope beyond just banking—it establishes an economy-wide data portability right for consumers under a single overarching legal, technical, and regulatory framework. Open banking is seen as just the beginning, with the energy sector already following an open data approach and the telecommunications sector ready to do the same.

Multiple government agencies collaborate on the development and oversight of the Consumer Data Rights— the Australian Treasury is the lead coordinator, while the Australian Competition and Consumer Commission is responsible for accrediting data recipients, the Data Standards Body defines the technical standards, and the Office of the Australian Information Commissioner handles complaints. A phased rollout required Australia's four major banks to share consumer data first, followed by smaller banks a year later. The government aims to expand the Consumer Data Rights into "open finance" by bringing nonbank lenders, merchant services, insurance, and superannuation under its purview. Moreover, future Consumer Data Rights enhancements will empower consumers to initiate actions like payments through accredited third parties, not just share data.

Regulator-Guided Jurisdictions

Hong Kong, China

The regulator, the Hong Kong Monetary Authority (HKMA), has not mandated open banking; instead, it is electing for a voluntary opt-in process and providing high-level guidance to assist financial institutions in agreeing on standards among themselves.[30] In 2018, the HKMA published a four-phase "Open API Framework" under its Smart Banking initiative. The first two phases, launched in 2019, facilitated banks making product information available via APIs and enabling customer applications through third parties. Phases 3 and 4, introduced progressively from late 2021 through 2022, aimed to provide access to account data and enable transactions/ payments through open APIs.

---

[30]   Kapronasia. 2022. Readiness of Legacy Systems for Open Banking in Asia Pacific. https://www.kapronasia.com/research/reports/legacy
-systems-open-banking-asia-pacific-epam.html.

However, progress on open banking adoption in Hong Kong, China has been relatively sluggish. A key obstacle is the lack of a formal accreditation framework—banks are understandably concerned about potential liabilities from sharing data with unvetted third parties. Furthermore, the HKMA left it to the major banks to determine data sharing standards, which deterred some fintechs. Compounding matters, banks have not seen strong commercial incentives to prioritize open API initiatives.

In response to the slow take-up, the HKMA has convened a group of 28 banks to explore pilot use cases. This effort falls under the Interbank Account Data Sharing Initiative announced in August 2023, aimed at fostering data-sharing among banks through APIs.[31]

The initiative focuses on bank-to-bank data sharing, targeting account aggregation and loan assessments for SMEs initially, with plans to extend to retail customers. Banks see this approach as less risky, given their common regulatory framework and operational standards. However, the initiative faces challenges, including complex consent management for SMEs and the potential for limited use cases if restricted to bank-to-bank sharing.

While the HKMA intends to eventually include fintechs in the open banking ecosystem, the current strategy may inadvertently slow the overall progress of open banking adoption in Hong Kong, China, by limiting initial use cases and dampening banks' motivation to invest in broader, more innovative projects.

Philippines

In the Philippines, progress on open finance was initially slow, but the country has accelerated its open finance initiatives in recent years. In June 2021, the Bangko Sentral ng Pilipinas (BSP), the central bank, published Circular No. 1122, establishing the Open Finance Framework. This initiative marked a significant step toward integrating open finance principles within the country's financial ecosystem. To facilitate the implementation of this framework, the BSP established the Open Finance Oversight Committee Transition Group, serving as an interim, industry-led governing entity.

In early 2022, the BSP unveiled a 3-year strategic road map, defining key priority actions to foster the development of open finance in line with the goals set out in the open finance framework. This comprehensive road map delineates a structured approach to expanding open finance services, enhancing collaboration among financial institutions, and fostering innovation in financial services.

In a push to further materialize the vision of the Open Finance Framework, in February 2023, the BSP invited financial institutions and third-party providers to engage in consultation about standards for the Philippine Open Finance Pilot. This pilot initiative, intended to test and refine open finance operations in a controlled environment, is to be closely monitored by the Open Finance Oversight Committee Transition Group. Additionally, the initiative receives support from the International Finance Corporation, underlining the collaborative effort and international backing behind the Philippines' move toward an open finance ecosystem. Much like Hong Kong, China, this is a voluntary undertaking by financial institutions to co-develop an open, interoperable, and scalable ecosystem. However, all participating institutions must adhere to the agreed-upon technical standards.

---

[31]   Hong Kong Monetary Authority. 2023. Interbank Account Data Sharing Pilot Programme. https://www.hkma.gov.hk/eng/news-and-media/press-releases/2023/12/20231221-3/.

This pilot program aims to assist the unbanked population, particularly those without proper documentation, in building financial profiles and credit histories. The platform will focus on giving consumers more control over their financial data and enabling access to a broader range of products and services from different companies.

For existing bank customers and micro, small, and medium-sized enterprises, the open finance platform would deliver more tailored financial solutions, such as personalized payment schemes and investment recommendations.

Across Asia and the Pacific, while there are growing efforts toward promoting open banking and open finance, the comprehensive implementation of open finance—in its truest sense, leveraging a wide array of financial data beyond simply banking data—is still emerging. This nascent state reflects both the challenges and opportunities that lie ahead. Challenges include creating cohesive regulatory frameworks and standards, ensuring data security and privacy, and building the necessary technological infrastructure. However, the opportunities for innovation, enhanced financial inclusion, and economic growth are immense, promising a transformative impact on the financial services landscape in Asia and the Pacific and beyond.

Lessons can be learned from the different approaches to open banking. While not all market participants may welcome a regulator-mandated approach like the one pursued by Australia, it does ensure progress. On the other hand, a market-led approach offers more flexibility but may come at the cost of slower adoption of open banking and open finance.

As Asia and the Pacific continues to navigate these complexities, the proliferation of open banking, and then its transition to true open finance, will require concerted efforts from regulators, market participants, and technology providers. This gradual evolution marks a significant step toward creating a more inclusive and interconnected financial ecosystem.

V. Key Lessons: Adapting Global Best Practices to Asia and the Pacific's Unique Landscape

Looking at the global development of open banking and open finance, emerging economies should keep a few lessons in mind as they consider open finance and its potential for financial inclusion.

Common standards. The standardization of APIs for open banking is crucial for ensuring interoperability across services and jurisdictions. In some jurisdictions, such as the UK and in the EU, such standards may be developed and mandated by the regulator. In others, regulators provide the necessary guidelines, leaving it to market players to adopt these as they deem fit. The regulator may then intervene to address the gaps in the market, as in Brazil's open banking project.

For instance, MAS in Singapore has actively promoted open banking by issuing a comprehensive, nonmandatory regulation and governance framework. Meanwhile, in the Philippines, "volunteer institutions" have been invited to participate in the collaborative development of technical and operational standards and arrangement of the Open Finance Pilot. Once agreed, participants in the pilot must comply with these standards, while institutions that are not participating in the pilot are exempt.

A potential drawback of imposing strict standards for open finance participation is the inadvertent exclusion of smaller players or those with legacy systems. Instead, guidelines that promote common principles and interoperable components without enforcing overly prescriptive formats can encourage broader participation and innovation across the financial ecosystem. Mandates also tend to bring reluctant participants to the table rather than allowing them to find the business and operational models that work.

Measures to ensure readiness. Both Singapore and the UK have implemented measures such as capacity building, regulatory sandboxes, and test environments. These initiatives enable entities unprepared for open banking to build their capabilities, preventing market exclusions and ensuring a smooth transition toward open finance. Such measures are particularly relevant for Asia's emerging markets, where financial institutions vary widely in technological readiness.

Drawing from the experience of the Philippines and Hong Kong, China, pilots are also important as they are designed for the financial sector to work collaboratively on a set of harmonized technical and operational standards within a prescribed framework. Financial institutions in the pilots are tasked with co-developing the open finance ecosystem, which can be done in a safe and secure "test and learn" environment.

Well-developed cybersecurity standards and practices. Given the increased risks associated with data sharing, regulators must emphasize cybersecurity strongly. Plans focusing on encryption, access controls, and continuous monitoring are paramount to safeguarding consumer data. This focus on security is critical for gaining consumer trust and fostering the adoption of open finance services across Asia. In addition, it is important to remove any ambiguity in where liability lies in the event of data breaches, cybercrime, and fraud.

Consumer protection and trust. Consumer protection and trust are pivotal in overcoming the adoption challenges faced by open banking, especially amid widespread public skepticism and safety concerns. Initial reactions in Europe were mixed, with significant worries about increased data breaches and fraud risks. This skepticism was not unfounded, as events like the Cambridge Analytica scandal had already heightened public awareness and concerns over data privacy. Recognizing the essential role of public understanding and trust, initiatives such as open banking UK's consumer-focused YouTube campaign aimed to demystify open banking, highlighting its benefits and safety measures to foster wider acceptance and participation.

To add on, high-profile scandals involving fintech firms, such as Wirecard and FTX Trading Ltd. (FTX), highlight the importance of robust safeguards protecting consumers, especially when it comes to handling financial data. In the Wirecard scandal, the German payment processor was accused of accounting fraud, while the collapse of the cryptocurrency exchange FTX in 2022 due to mishandling of customer funds and lack of corporate controls dealt a major blow to trust in the crypto industry. These cases, where fintech firms promising advanced technology were revealed to have serious governance issues and fraud, highlight the need for transparency and robust safeguards to protect consumers and investors.

Incentivizing participation for market-led regimes. The success of open finance in market-led regimes, such as Singapore, often hinges on creating incentives for participation. These may include regulatory reliefs, grants, or support programs for fintech innovation. For example, the Monetary Authority of Singapore launched the MAS Financial Sector Technology and Innovation Innovation Acceleration Track program, which provides up to 50% funding support for experimentation, development, and dissemination of nascent innovative technologies in the financial services sector.[32]

Inclusive policy frameworks. Policy frameworks governing open finance should mandate mechanisms like representational audits and impact assessments to ensure that the systems do not perpetuate biases or exclusions. The Open Banking Standard in the UK mandates the use of ethical design principles and the consideration of potential biases in the development of open banking solutions. These guidelines include provisions for grievance redressal mechanisms and ongoing stakeholder consultations.

Furthermore, policy frameworks can mandate the establishment of independent oversight bodies or advisory councils composed of representatives from diverse communities, consumer advocacy groups, and industry experts.

Building cross-border synergies. Open finance's potential to transcend national boundaries highlights the importance of cross-border collaborations, particularly in regions like ASEAN. The ASEAN+3 (Association of Southeast Asian Nations plus the People's Republic of China, Japan, and the Republic of Korea) has made significant strides in deepening financial cooperation, with initiatives like the ASEAN+3 Macro-structural Framework and Program Toolkit developed by the Working Group 2 (WG2) with support from ASEAN+3 Macroeconomic Research Office (AMRO). Additionally, it has focused on enhancing regional policy coordination on fintech and introducing the Open Banking System as an area for technical cooperation in the region.[33]

---

[32]   Monetary Authority of Singapore. 2024. MAS FSTI Innovation Acceleration – Early Innovation. https://www.mas.gov.sg/development/fintech/mas-fsti-innovation-acceleration-track---early-innovation.

[33]   ASEAN+3 Macroeconomic Research Office. 2023. Joint Statement of the 26th ASEAN+3 Finance Ministers' and Central Bank Governors' Meeting. Incheon, Republic of Korea. 2 May 2023. https://amro-asia.org/joint-statement-of-the-26th-asean3-finance-ministers-and-central-bank-governors-meeting-incheon-korea-2-may-2023/.

Several ASEAN+3 countries have launched initiatives for cross-border Quick Response (QR) code payments and real-time payment system linkages, facilitating seamless transactions across borders. Malaysia and Indonesia linked their systems in 2023 for businesses and individuals, while Thailand connected its PromptPay with systems in Viet Nam, Indonesia, Malaysia, Japan, and between 2020 and 2022 to facilitate real-time QR code payments. Notably, Singapore and Thailand launched the world's first real-time cross-border payment linkage between PayNow and PromptPay in 2021.[34] These efforts underscore the region's commitment to fostering an integrated financial ecosystem, enabling greater financial inclusion and economic growth through open finance initiatives.

By analyzing global best practices and adapting them to local contexts, Asia and the Pacific economies can navigate the complexities of implementing open finance. Learning from the successes and challenges of pioneers like Singapore and the UK, the region can develop a tailored approach that addresses its unique market needs, regulatory environments, and technological landscapes, paving the way for a more inclusive and innovative financial future.

---

[34] World Economic Forum. 2023. *Shaping the Future of Cross-Border Fast Payment Systems: Revolutionizing Transactions in South-East Asia.* https://www3.weforum.org/docs/WEF_Shaping%20the_Future_of_Cross-Border_Fast_Payment_Systems_2023.pdf.

VI. Technology and Cultural Considerations in Open Finance

The adoption of open finance within Asia and the Pacific globally necessitates careful consideration of technological and cultural factors. These considerations are vital for ensuring that the transition toward more open, interoperable financial systems respects the diversity of existing systems and cultural contexts, fostering inclusivity and sustainability.

Blending Modern Tech with Traditional Systems

While open banking and open finance present a vast opportunity for banks to innovate and expand their reach, their legacy core banking systems pose a significant obstacle. These systems, often built in the 1970s and 1980s, were designed for reliability in a pre-digital era. While robust and stable, their closed architecture and incompatibility with modern development approaches make them ill-suited for open banking/finance's demands.

Legacy systems also struggle to integrate with modern infrastructure and platforms, limiting operational efficiency and the ability to leverage advanced technologies like AI for data analysis and personalized customer experiences. While cloud infrastructure offers scalability and flexibility to handle growing volumes of data and transactions, open banking and open finance initiatives can be implemented in both cloud and on-premises environments.

The key challenge lies in the ability of legacy systems to seamlessly integrate with new technologies and platforms, regardless of the deployment model. On-premise solutions with robust integration capabilities can also leverage AI and other advanced analytics tools for data analysis and personalized services. However, cloud-based environments often provide easier access to scalable computing resources and pre-existing toolsets, enabling faster innovation and deployment of new services.

Simply put, legacy core banking systems' complex, inflexible information technology architectures are not designed for the flexibility, agility, and scalability required by open banking. Despite efforts to adapt these legacy systems through various fixes and enabling API communication, the solutions are often suboptimal, primarily because these core systems, often based on outdated technology and programming, are crucial to a bank's operations and difficult to upgrade without risking significant disruptions.

Integrating an open API architecture, therefore, necessitates a nuanced approach to technology adoption, one that balances innovation with the realities of existing financial infrastructures. To tackle this challenge, financial institutions have centered their efforts on three distinct approaches to integrating the requisite open finance infrastructure with their existing legacy systems (footnote 34):

(i) **Rip-and-replace.** This approach completely overhauls existing systems in favor of new technologies. While potentially offering a clean slate for innovation, it requires substantial investment and risk. Financial institutions can either replace their core systems with a traditional enterprise or a cloud-based core banking system.
(ii) **Gradual journey-led transition.** Financial institutions may opt for a phased approach, gradually integrating new technologies and processes with existing legacy systems. This method allows learning and adaptation but can be slow and complex.
(iii) **Greenfield cloud-native stack.** Some institutions choose to build new, cloud-native platforms from scratch, parallel to their legacy systems. This approach can foster innovation and agility but may result in siloed operations.

Data Ethics in a Diverse Cultural Context

In the evolving landscape of open finance, integrating cultural considerations forms the backbone of a truly inclusive and globally responsive financial ecosystem. As financial services extend their reach across borders, the importance of adapting to and respecting local cultural nuances cannot be overstated. This adaptability involves a refined approach beyond mere compliance with local customs; it requires a deep understanding of the diverse ways in which different cultures approach financial matters such as savings, investment, borrowing, and even their fundamental trust in financial institutions.

The varying preferences across cultures, ranging from a predilection for cash transactions to a rapid embrace of digital payments, necessitate that open finance initiatives be versatile, offering a suite of services that resonate with and respect these local behaviors and attitudes. Moreover, the success of these services hinges on effective communication, ensuring accessibility in the local languages, and aligning marketing strategies with the community's values, aspirations, and concerns to foster engagement and trust.

Data ethics and privacy concerns are perceived differently across cultural contexts. Societies with a communal orientation may be more open to data sharing for collective benefits, while those prioritizing individual rights may place greater emphasis on consent and personal data protection. Regulatory and ethical frameworks must align with the cultural fabric of each region to foster trust and engagement.

Inclusion and accessibility form another pillar of cultural consideration in open finance, emphasizing the need for interfaces and financial products that are accessible to all, regardless of their financial literacy, technological proficiency, or physical abilities. This inclusivity extends to acknowledging and addressing barriers that may stem from cultural practices, such as traditional gender roles or a general distrust in formal banking systems.

Designing open finance platforms and services requires thoughtful consideration of cultural diversity, from an app's aesthetics to the diversity of financial products offered. For example, this could mean incorporating Islamic banking principles in predominantly Muslim countries or facilitating group savings features in cultures that value financial collectivism.

Cultural sensitivity in the realm of open finance is not merely an ethical imperative but a strategic one, enabling the expansion of financial services in a way that is respectful, inclusive, and effective. By weaving cultural considerations into the fabric of open finance, the financial sector can achieve a more equitable, understanding, and impactful global financial ecosystem that is truly reflective of the diverse world it serves.

The evolution of open finance not only heralds a new era of financial services but also sets the stage for a redefined relationship between financial entities, technology giants, and policymakers. The broader implications of this shift suggest a landscape where strategic directions are governed by innovation, ethical considerations, and a collaborative approach to regulation.

Future Roles of Financial Entities and Tech Giants

Open finance and open banking aim to create a more collaborative and interoperable financial ecosystem, but many traditional banks are hesitant to embrace this shift. The main concern revolves around losing their competitive edge and eroding their profitability by sharing data and services with third parties.

However, banks may have little choice but to adapt as customer expectations evolve alongside better experiences due to technological improvement, more choices, and accessible financial products. Customers are seeking seamless integration of financial services into their daily lives, and if traditional banks fail to deliver, competitors will seize the opportunity. Banks willing to modernize have a chance to tap into new growth opportunities and distribution channels. Still, they must find a balance between embracing open finance and protecting their competitive advantages.

For traditional financial institutions, the transition to open finance may necessitate a significant cultural change within the organization. This shift involves embracing API integration as a core component of their business models, allowing for seamless data sharing and collaboration with third-party providers.

Additionally, financial institutions must invest in oversight mechanisms to ensure data privacy and security, alongside internal restructuring efforts aimed at leveraging data synergies.

As tech companies expand their footprint in the financial services sector, they face critical challenges related to privacy invasion and market domination. Addressing these concerns requires a commitment to ethical data practices and a willingness to work within regulatory frameworks designed to protect consumer interests and promote fair competition. Tech firms must prioritize transparency, consent, and user control over data while also fostering innovation that benefits the broader financial ecosystem without compromising on privacy or security.

Policymaking for an Ethically Driven Open Finance Future

The open finance ecosystem needs to be sufficiently attractive for financial institutions, third-party providers, and customers to participate in a sustainable manner. To foster an ethically driven open finance future, policymakers play a crucial role in shaping the regulatory landscape to encourage innovation while ensuring consumer protection, data privacy, and financial stability. To achieve this, the frameworks need to incorporate the following conditions (footnote 9):

(i)   provide the right incentives to attract financial institutions and third-party providers;
(ii)   build customer confidence in the safety, reliability, and fairness of the framework, and enable them to effectively reap tangible benefits from such frameworks; and
(iii)   enable minimum technical interoperability for data sharing (alongside regulatory interoperability among different frameworks).

Key recommendations for policymakers on how to approach the development and governance of open finance include:

Develop Comprehensive Regulatory Frameworks

Policymakers should focus on creating comprehensive regulatory frameworks that address the unique challenges and opportunities of open finance. These frameworks should cover critical areas such as data privacy, consumer rights, cybersecurity, and the ethical use of financial data.

Additionally, regulators and policymakers can play a proactive role in shaping the open finance landscape by signaling the specific types of applications or services they would like to see in the market, such as personal financial management tools. By setting clear guidelines, standards, and targeted objectives, regulators can not only provide a stable foundation for the growth of open finance but also steer market forces toward achieving intended outcomes that might not be realized through market forces alone. This approach, coupled with robust consumer protection measures and security protocols, can ensure innovations in the open finance sector are consumer-friendly and secure.

Foster an Ecosystem of Collaboration

Encouraging collaboration among all stakeholders, including traditional financial institutions, fintech startups, technology providers, and consumer advocacy groups, is vital. Policymakers can facilitate forums, working groups, and partnerships that bring together diverse perspectives to inform policy development. This collaborative approach can help identify common goals, address potential conflicts, and leverage collective expertise to advance open finance.

Regulators can promote innovation by setting up regulatory sandboxes and pilots. These allow fintech companies and financial institutions to test innovative products, services, and business models in a controlled environment under regulatory supervision. Sandboxes serve as a bridge between regulation and innovation, providing valuable insights into how new technologies operate within regulatory frameworks and identifying areas where regulations may need to be adapted to support innovation.

The BSP has embraced a regulatory sandbox approach to oversee fintech innovation. As part of this framework, the ongoing open finance pilot is being conducted within the open finance regulatory sandbox. Members of the Open Finance Oversight Committee Technical Group are responsible for developing initial policies and standards, as well as supporting pilot projects within this sandbox. Each member represents their respective industry, ensuring a comprehensive and collaborative approach to regulation and implementation.[35]

Invest in Digital Literacy and Financial Education

As open finance relies heavily on digital platforms and technologies, investing in digital literacy and financial education becomes imperative. Policymakers should support initiatives that enhance the public's understanding of open finance services, the benefits of data sharing, and the importance of data security. Equipping consumers with the knowledge to make informed decisions about their financial data will not only empower them but also foster greater trust in open finance systems.

Ensure International Cooperation and Harmonization

Open finance is a global movement, and its success depends on the ability of systems to operate across borders. Policymakers should work toward international cooperation to harmonize open finance standards and regulations. This includes agreements on data sharing, consumer protection, and cybersecurity measures. International collaboration through forums and platforms such as the Berlin Group, Open Banking Expo,[36] and the ASEAN Financial Innovation Network can also facilitate the sharing of technical know-how and best-practices on cross-border payments and financial services, making it easier for consumers and businesses to operate globally.

Implement Strategic Phases for Rollout

Recognizing the complexity of open finance, a phased approach to implementation can allow the financial ecosystem to adapt gradually. Starting with sectors where data sharing can have immediate benefits, such as banking, before moving to insurance, investments, and beyond, this allows each segment of the financial industry time to adjust and prepare for the changes open finance brings.

By adhering to these recommendations, policymakers can create a conducive environment for the growth of open finance, ensuring that it remains consumer-centric, secure, and innovative. Open finance can achieve its full potential in transforming the financial landscape through careful planning, collaboration, and a commitment to ethical principles.

---

[35]   BSP. Open Finance PH. https://www.bsp.gov.ph/Pages/InclusiveFinance/Open%20Finance/Open%20Finance.aspx.
[36]   The Berlin Group. About. https://www.berlin-group.org/; Open Banking Expo. https://www.openbankingexpo.com/.

The *Redefining Financial Ecosystems in Asia and the Pacific* report's journey through the evolving landscape of open finance highlights a compelling vision for the future of financial services—a vision that is inclusive, efficient, and ripe with innovation. As we delve deeper into the intricacies of integrating modern technology with traditional financial systems and navigate the vast cultural landscapes that shape financial behaviors worldwide, the call for a collaborative and ethical financial ecosystem becomes increasingly clear.

With its promise to democratize access to financial services, open finance stands as a beacon of hope for broadening economic participation. It challenges the status quo, tearing down the barriers that have historically excluded the unbanked and underbanked from the financial narrative.

This potential will only be realized through the efforts of a wide array of stakeholders. Incumbent financial institutions are urged to pivot toward a more open architecture, embracing APIs and leveraging data to unlock new synergies. Meanwhile, technology firms, as emerging powerhouses in the financial domain, are tasked with navigating the fine line between innovation, compliance, risk management, and ethical responsibility, particularly in areas of data privacy and market influence. Policymakers, for their part, are instrumental in sculpting the regulatory frameworks that will underpin this new era, ensuring that the march toward innovation does not come at the cost of consumer trust or systemic stability.

The narrative woven through this exploration underscores a critical transition—from the foundations of open banking to open finance and eventually to the much broader concept of open data. This evolution demands more than mere technological interoperability; it calls for a cultural shift toward openness, consumer-centricity, and an unwavering commitment to ethical principles. Through such a transformation, the financial sector is poised to offer a more integrated, personalized, and inclusive array of services.

The recommendations and strategic insights offered chart a course for navigating the complexities of open finance. From advocating for comprehensive toolkits for regulators to fostering cross-border collaborations, the path forward involves a concerted effort to harmonize technological advancements with ethical considerations. Such a balanced approach is essential for nurturing an open finance ecosystem that is resilient, reflects collective values, and is appropriate for the country's specific context.

Glossary

Account aggregation

A service that consolidates information from multiple financial accounts into a single view for the user.

Account information service provider

A third-party provider that accesses and aggregates a customer's account information from multiple banks with the customer's consent.

Account-to-account payments

Direct bank transfers between accounts without intermediaries.

Alternative credit scoring

Methods of assessing creditworthiness using nontraditional data sources to include underserved populations.

API aggregators

Companies that consolidate data from multiple APIs to provide a single access point for data users.

Application programming interfaces

Sets of rules or protocols that allow software applications to communicate with each other to exchange data, features, and functionality.

Artificial intelligence

Technology that uses data to provide personalized financial advice and automate processes, enhancing customer experiences.

Biometric authentication

The use of biological characteristics (like fingerprints or facial features) to verify identity.

Blockchain

A decentralized, digital ledger technology used to record transactions across multiple computers.

Buy now, pay later

A type of short-term financing that allows consumers to make purchases and pay for them at a future date.

Chargeback

A demand by a credit card provider for a retailer to make good the loss on a fraudulent or disputed transaction.

Cloud-native platforms

Software platforms designed to operate in cloud environments, offering scalability and flexibility.

Consent management	Obtaining, recording, and managing user consent for data sharing and processing, ensuring compliance with privacy regulations.
Consumer Data Rights	Legislation in Australia that allows consumers to access and control their data held by businesses.
Cross-border synergies	Collaborative efforts and interactions between different countries or regions to enhance the effectiveness and efficiency of systems or processes.
Cybersecurity	Protecting systems, networks, and data from digital attacks, which is crucial for maintaining trust in financial systems.
Data aggregation	Gathering and combining data from multiple sources into a single, summarized form.
Data owners	Individuals or businesses who own the financial data and provide consent for its use within the open finance ecosystem.
Data providers	Entities that hold a customer's financial information and can share it securely with other participants in the ecosystem with customer consent.
Data users	Fintech companies or third-party service providers that leverage shared consumer data to offer innovative financial products and services.
Electronic know your customer	Verifying a customer's identity electronically.
Embedded finance	The integration of financial services or tools within nonfinancial products, services, or technologies.
Financial inclusion	Ensuring access to financial services for all individuals, particularly underserved or marginalized groups, to promote economic development and reduce poverty.
Financial service providers	Organizations that offer financial services like banking, investment, and insurance.
Fintech	Short for "financial technology," referring to companies that use technology to provide financial services.
General Data Protection Regulation	A comprehensive data protection law in the European Union that emphasizes data privacy and consumer control over personal information.
Inclusive growth	Economic growth that is distributed fairly across society and creates opportunities for all individuals to participate in the economic process.
Interoperability	The ability of different systems and organizations to work together and exchange information seamlessly.

Know-your-customer — A process used by financial institutions to verify the identity of their clients and assess potential risks.

Legacy banking systems — Traditional banking systems that may be outdated or inflexible, often presenting challenges for integration with modern technologies.

Machine learning — A subset of artificial intelligence that enables systems to learn and improve from experience without being explicitly programmed.

Microinsurance — Insurance products designed for low-income populations, typically characterized by low premiums and coverage limits.

Open API — APIs that are publicly available for developers to access and use.

Open banking — A system where banks share consumer data with third-party providers through APIs, with customer consent, to create new or improved financial products and services.

Open data — A concept extending open finance to include data from various sectors such as health care, utilities, and social media, promoting innovation and competition.

Open finance — An extension of open banking that includes a broader range of financial services and data-sharing capabilities, such as mortgages, investments, pensions, and insurance.

Parallel, cloud-native platforms — New systems designed to operate alongside existing ones, utilizing cloud technology to offer scalability and flexibility.

Payment initiation service provider — A third-party provider that initiates payments on behalf of customers directly from their bank accounts.

Payment Services Directive 2 — A European Union directive aimed at promoting innovation and competition in retail payments, enhancing payment security, and protecting consumer data.

Quick response code (QR code) — A type of matrix barcode that contains information about the item to which it is attached.

Regulatory frameworks — Sets of guidelines and rules established by authorities to govern the implementation and operation of systems like open banking and open finance .

Regulatory sandbox — A framework set up by a regulator that allows fintech startups and other innovators to conduct live experiments in a controlled environment under regulatory supervision.

Smart onboarding — Advanced processes for enrolling new customers using digital tools to streamline and simplify the registration process.

Software as a Service	A software licensing and delivery model in which software is licensed on a subscription basis and is centrally hosted.
Technical standards	Established norms and requirements for technical systems and processes to ensure compatibility and interoperability.
Thin-file	A credit report with little or no credit history.
Third-party providers	External companies that access consumer banking data to offer additional financial services or products.
Underbanked	Individuals or businesses that have limited access to mainstream financial services that are normally offered by retail banks.
Unstructured supplementary service data	A protocol used by cellular telephones to communicate with the mobile network operator's computers.

www.ingramcontent.com/pod-product-compliance
Lightning Source LLC
LaVergne TN
LVHW071454180726
843512LV00018B/1380